Coney Island

The Decline & Death
of an American Icon

Featuring the photography
and notes of Michael Malott

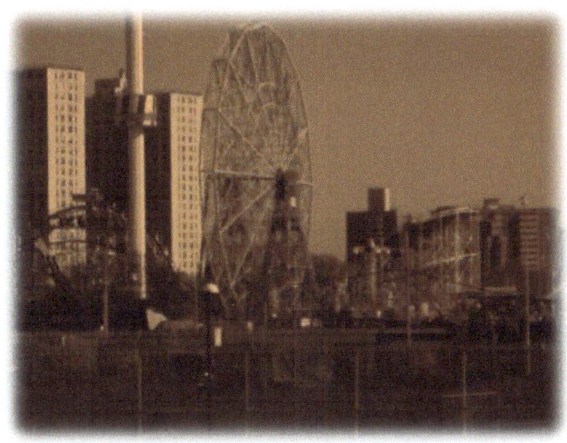

The History of Coney Island

I never made it to Coney Island as a kid. But, I definitely knew of it growing up in Michigan. Our family vacations consisted of a yearly visit to Miami and Ft. Myers, Florida and an annual summer trip to Acton, Massachusetts and the Cape. I knew of Coney Island, but it always was a myth to me.

Now years later, I caught wind of news of new developments for Coney Island. The city turned the lease over to an aggressive multi-billion dollar corporation who has big plans for the future of Coney Island. A future that is sure to destroy the unique feel and personality of Coney Island. Sure enough when all the independent businesses leases expired on November 1st, 2010, all but two received notice that after years of being in business on the boardwalk, that they had 15 days to vacate. The two lucky survivors, a boutique and gift shop called Lola Starr and of course, Nathan's Hot Dogs. For fear of the destruction of Coney Island I took my son two days later to Coney Island. The purpose, that my son see Coney Island the way it was, in his lifetime.

All I could think of is how Asbury Park let the legendary Palace Amusements building meet a wrecking ball to its tragic end, a move that will haunt Asbury Park for eternity. But, Coney Island has that eerie allure, the charm, character, and vibe unlike anywhere else I know.

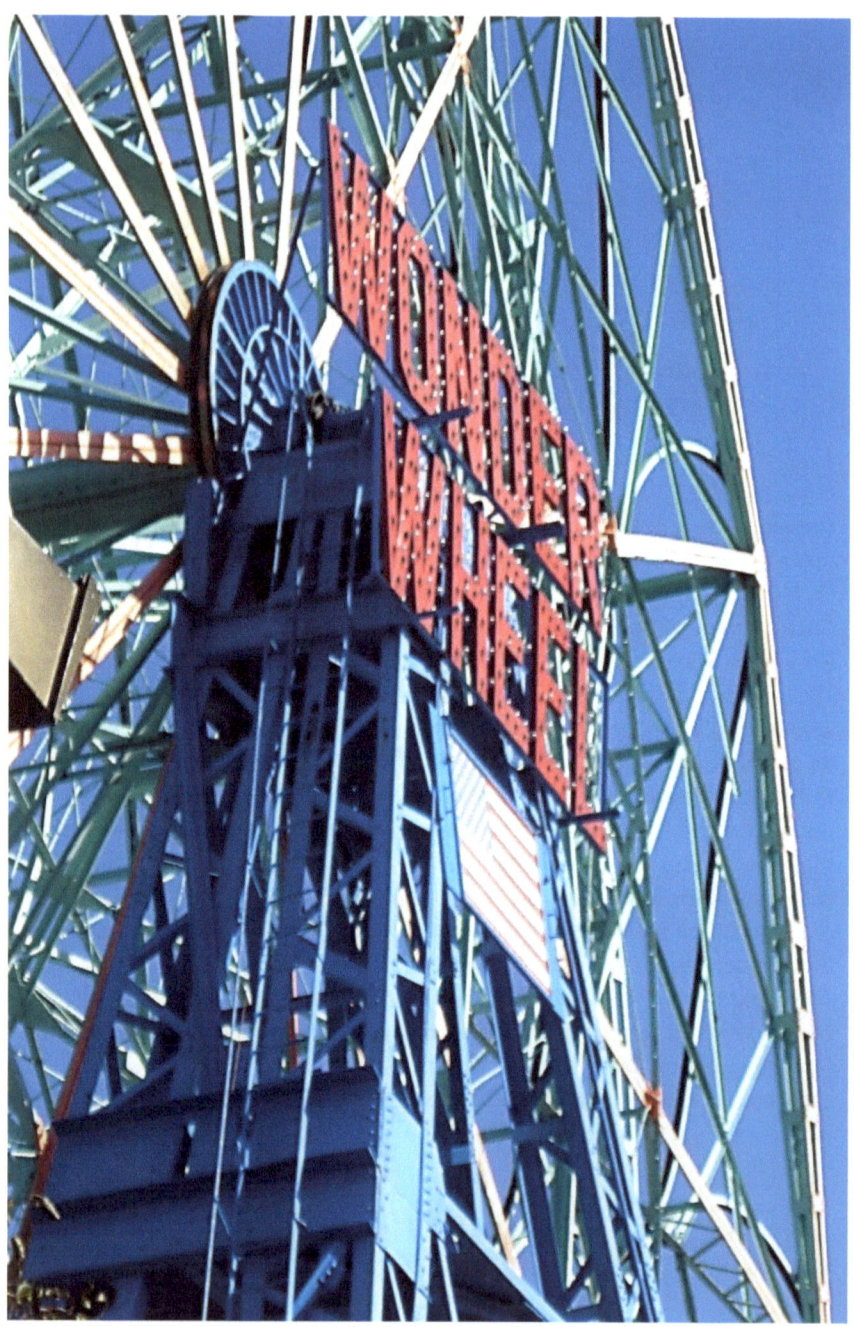

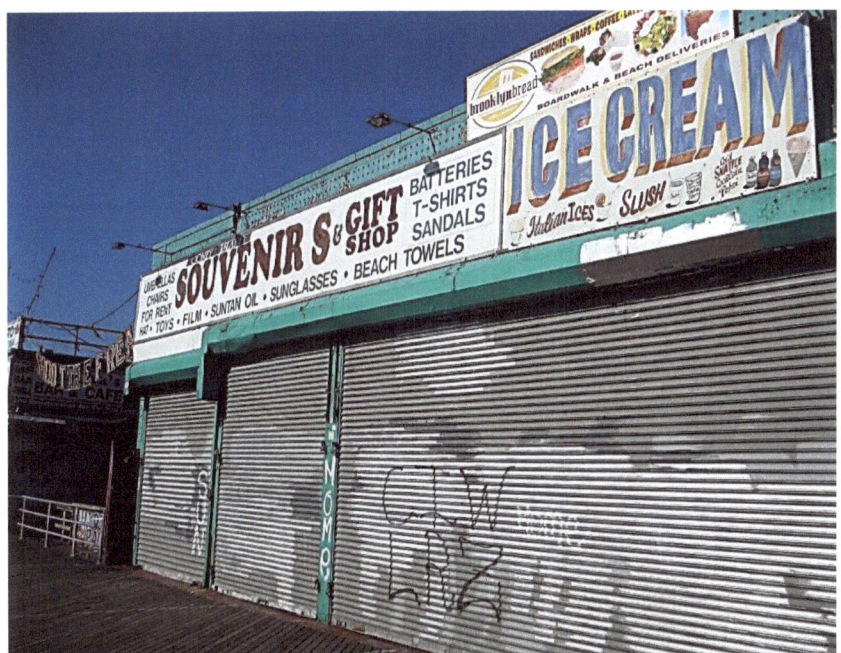

Souvenir stores and mom and pop eateries now a thing of the past and forced to give way to the corporate Starbucks and sports bars.

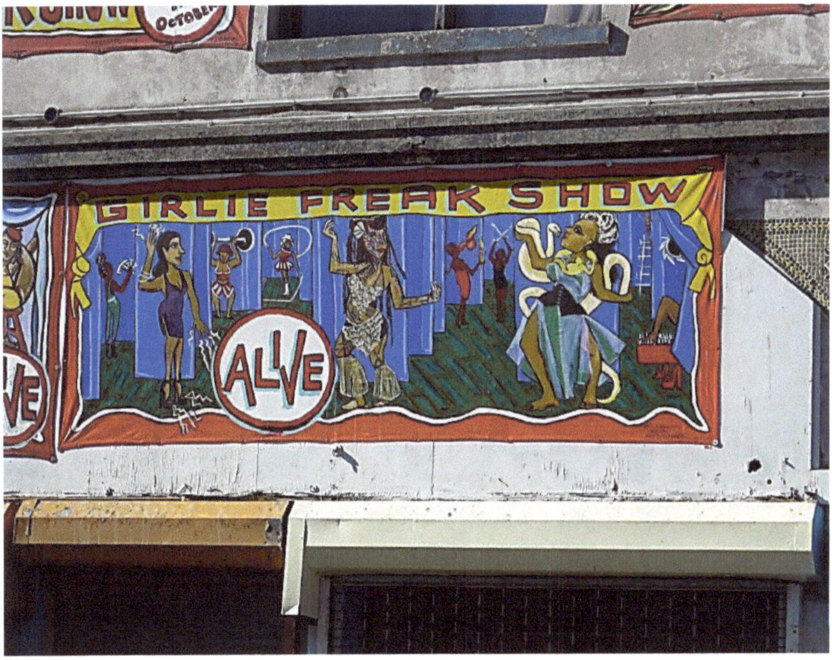

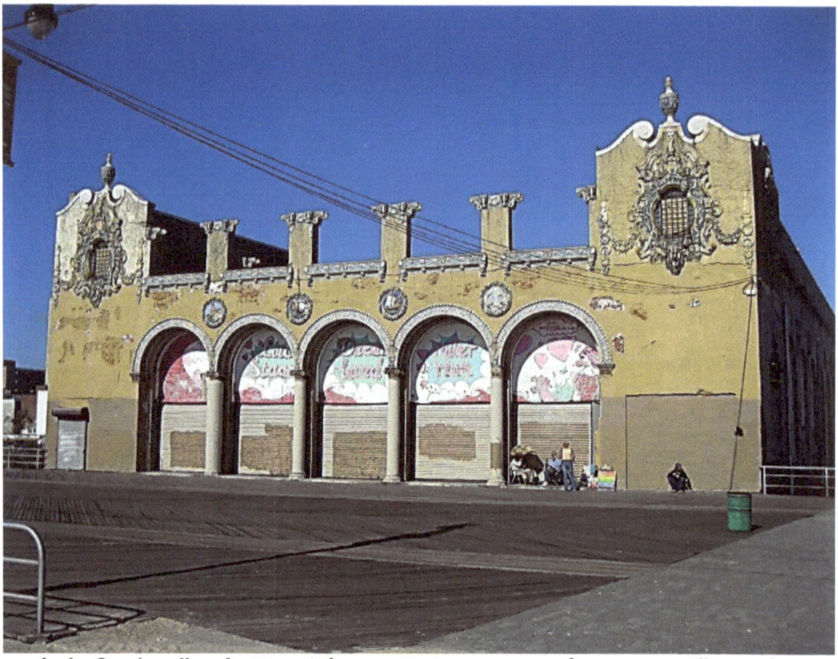

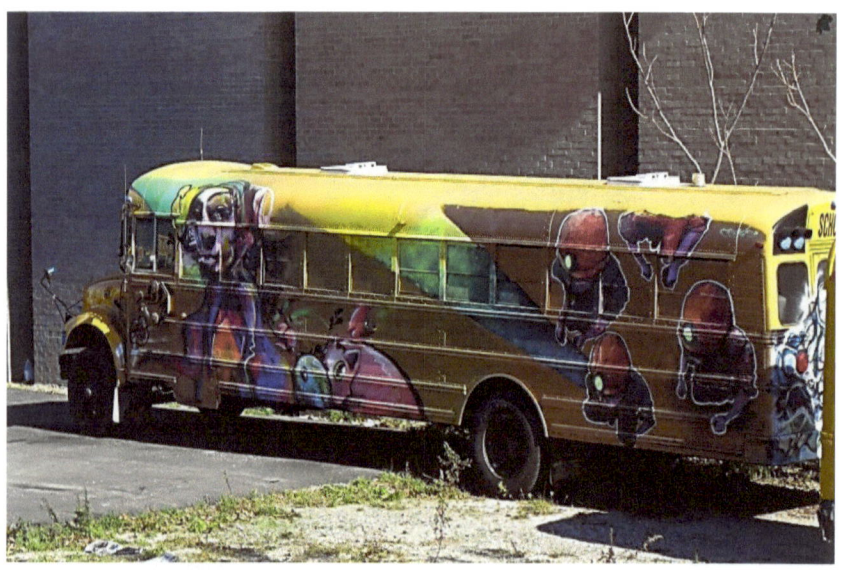

Lola Star's roller skating rink, now just a memory for many, will soon be replaced with 5000 new housing units and modern corporate retail stores. The boardwalk will soon become the "cementwalk".

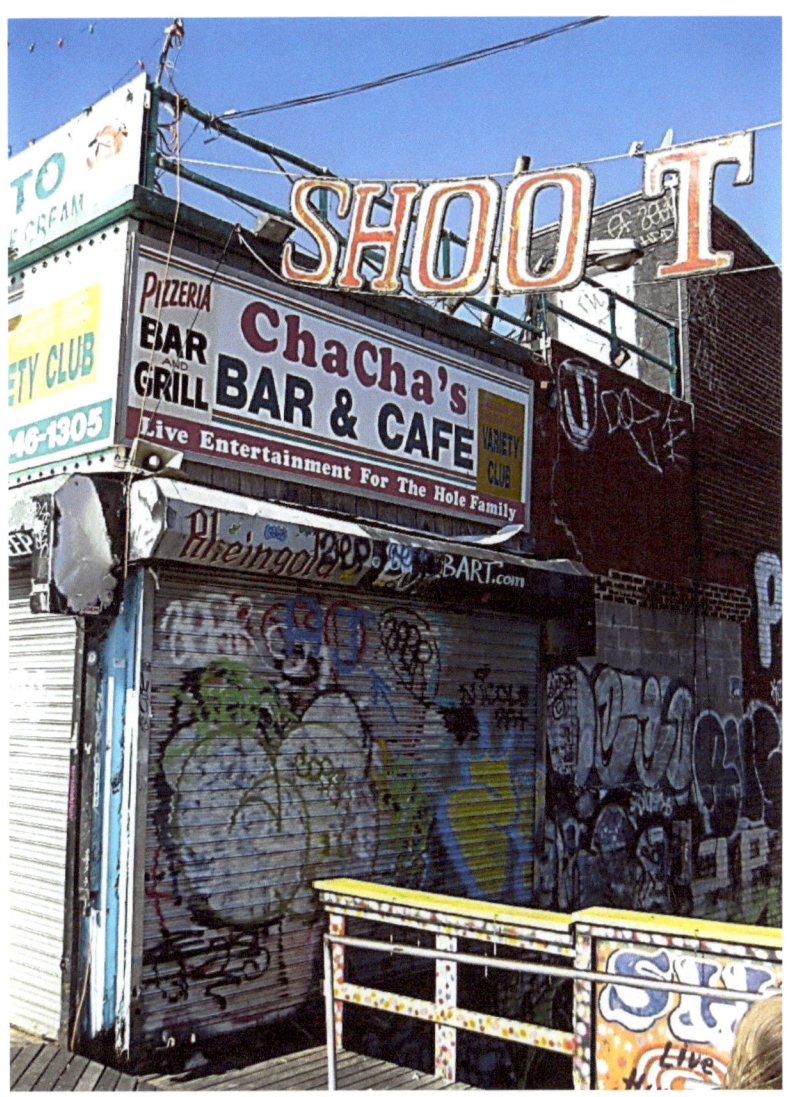

Coney Island has always featured the strange and odd. Sideshows have always been a part of its heritage since its earliest days. Here you would find the bearded lady, pretzel man, the world's strongest man, and lobster boy.

The circus sideshows once thrived in Coney Island's eccentric boardwalk atmosphere. This will all become a thing of the past as Coney Island heads for a huge redevelopment featuring a state of the art recreational area, housing units, corporate retailers, sports bars, and sit down restaurants. This all at the hands of the city's new tenant, Central Amusement International who just signed a lease to control the 6.2 acres of Coney Island for the next ten years.

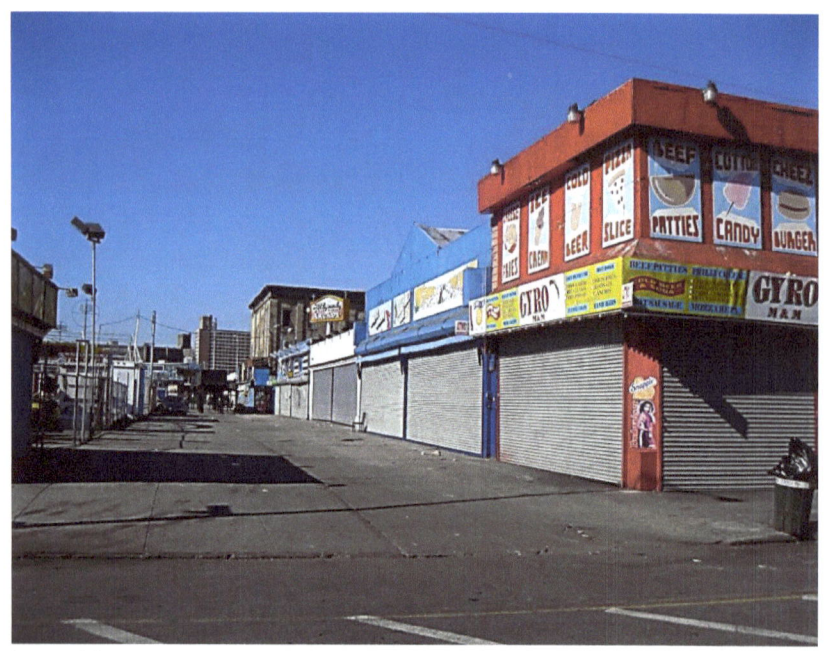

Central Amusements gave tenants just 15 days to vacate stores that some had occupied for over 60 years.

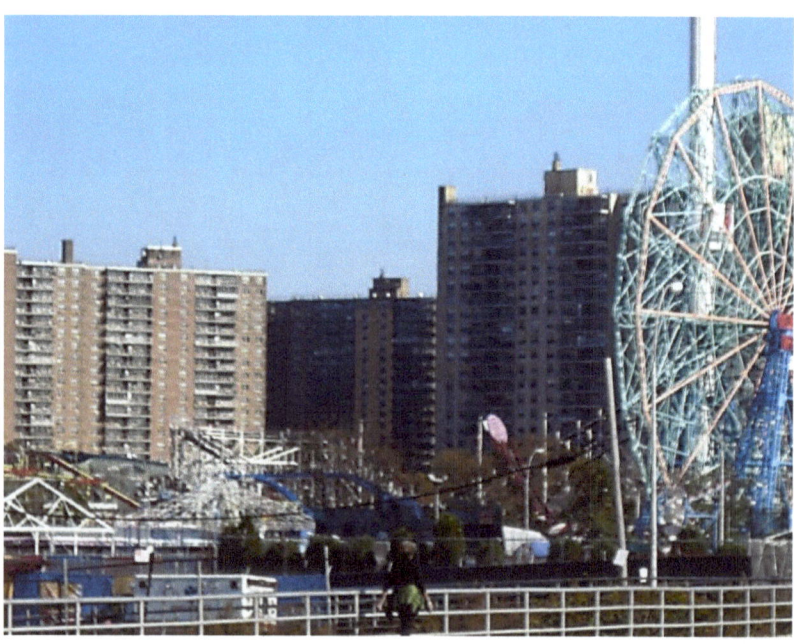

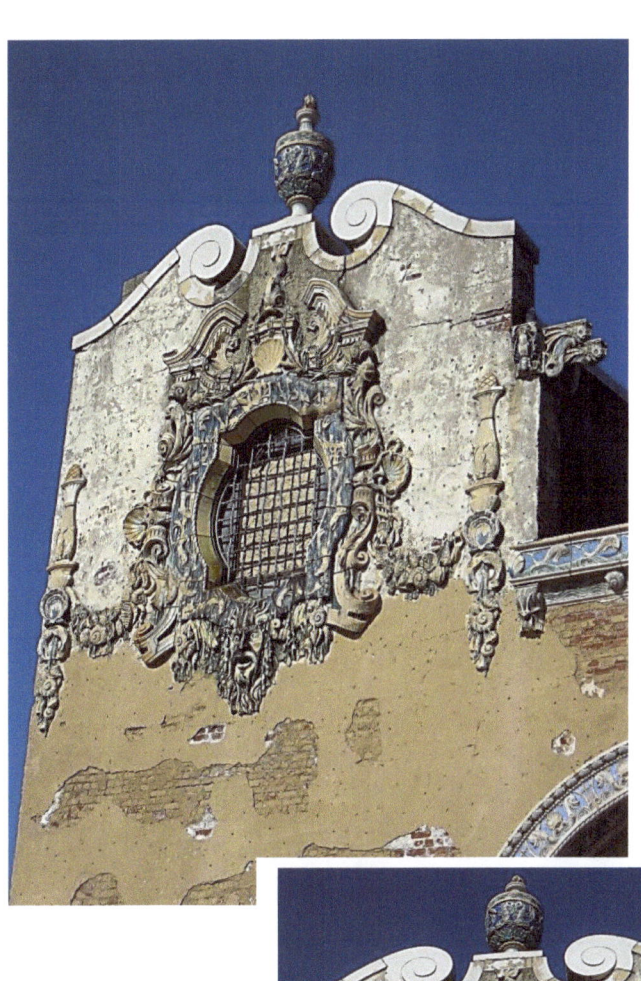

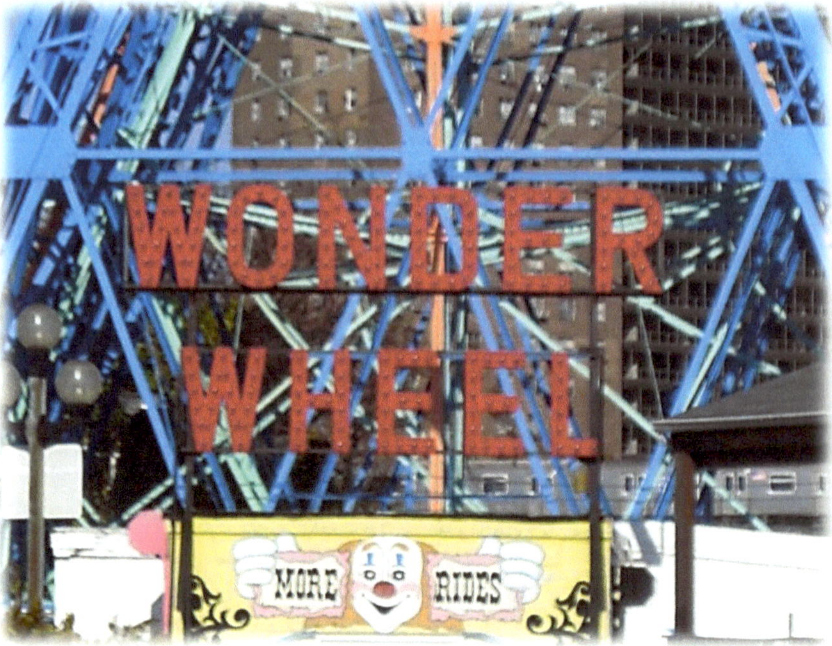

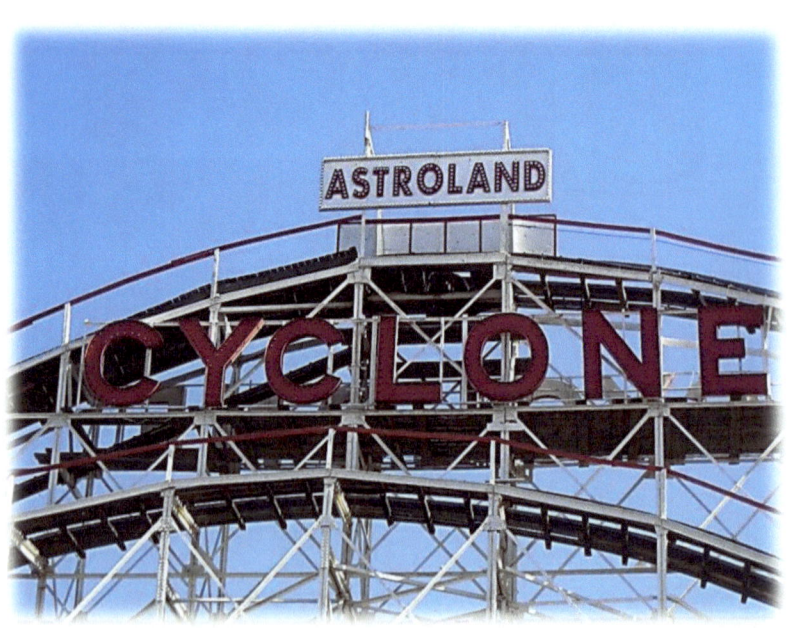

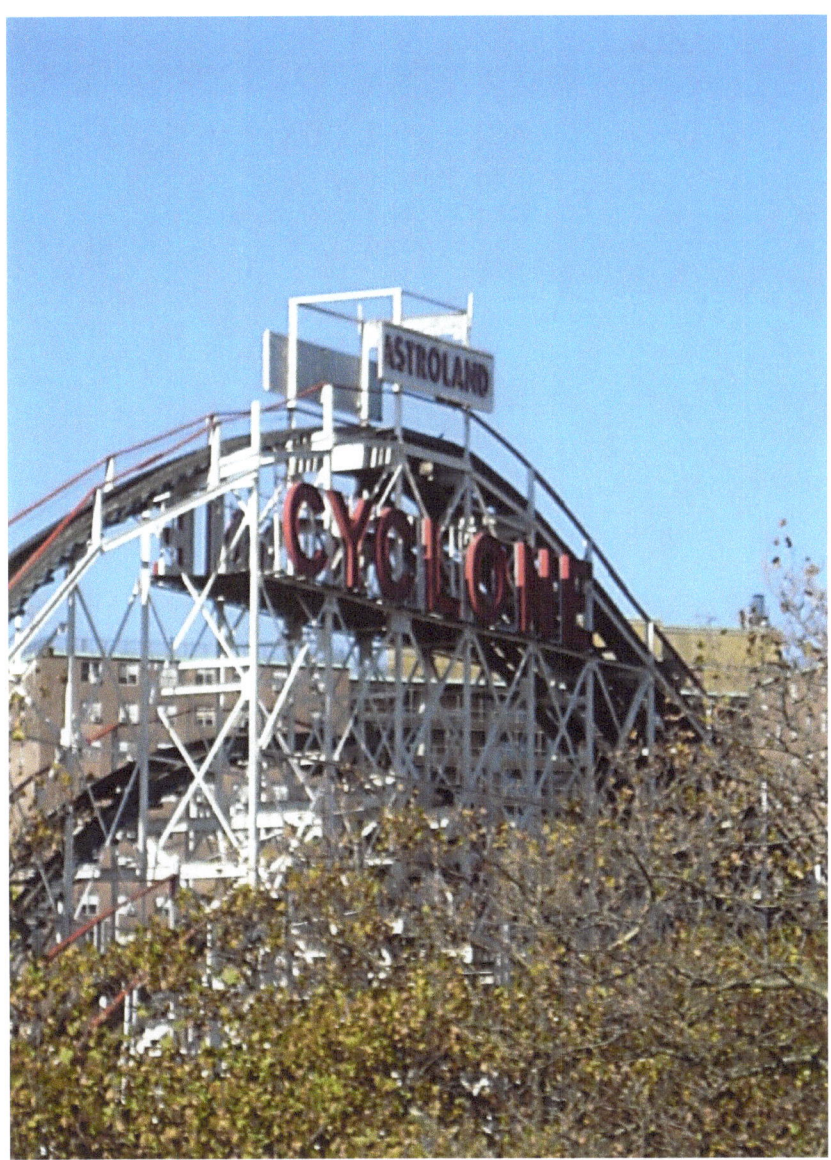

The Cyclone Roller Coaster has been a mainstay in Coney Island since its construction in 1927. It was By the 1960s, attendance at Coney Island had lowered. By 1968, the Cyclone was deteriorating and it was shut down in 1969. In 1971, the Cyclone was bought by the city of New York for one million dollars. The ride was condemned in 1972, and the coaster was leased to the Astroland amusement park for $57,000 per year. Astroland's owners had the ride refurbished, and it reopened on July 3, 1975. It became a national historic landmark in 1991.

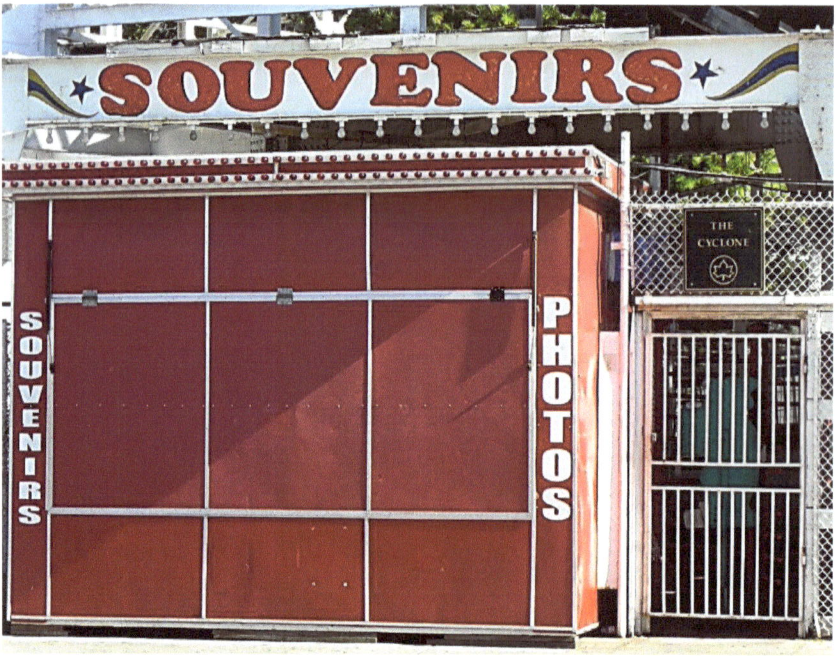
SOUVENIRS
SOUVENIRS
PHOTOS
THE CYCLONE

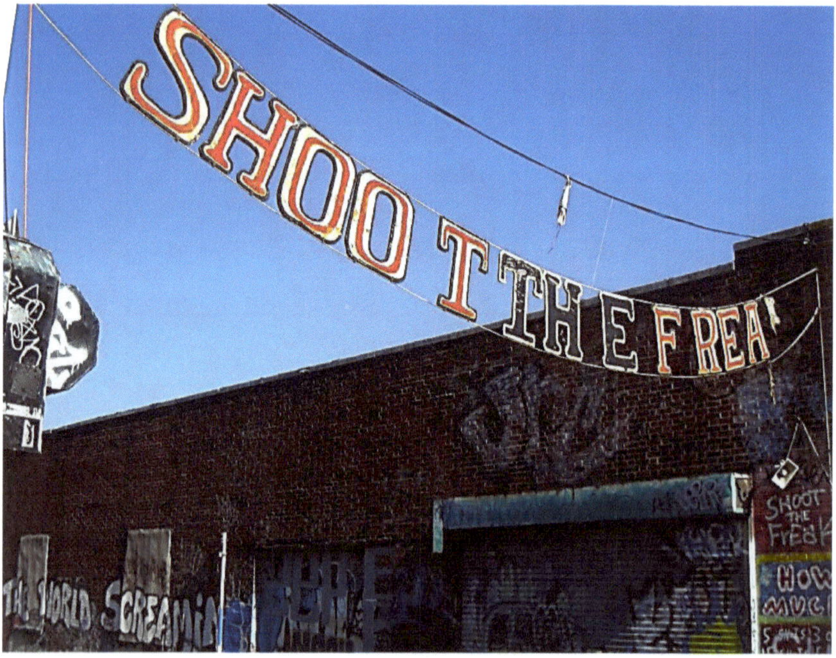
SHOO T THE FREA
SHOOT THE FREAK

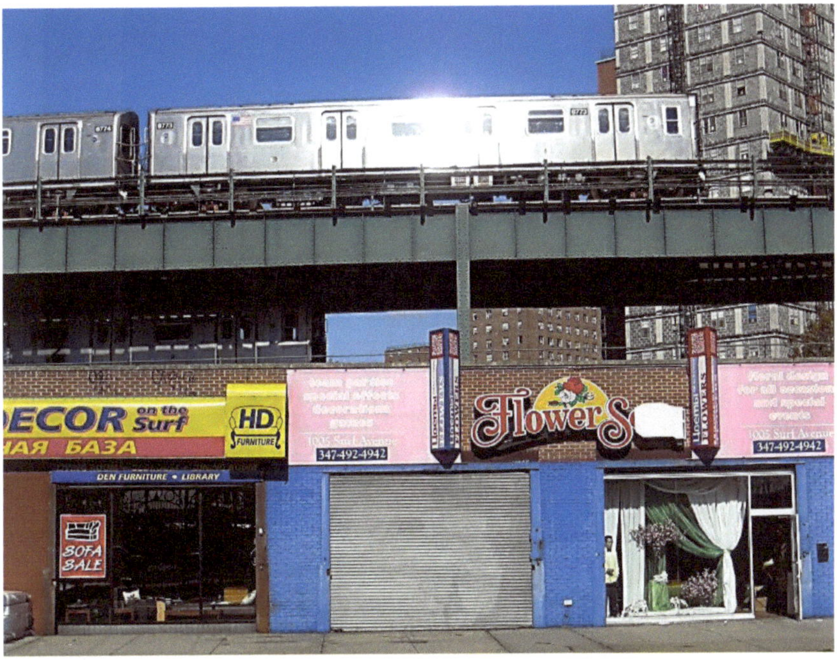
DECOR on the Surf
НАЯ БАЗА
HD FURNITURE
DEN FURNITURE • LIBRARY
SOFA SALE
1005 Surf Avenue
347-492-4942
1005 Surf Avenue
347-492-4942

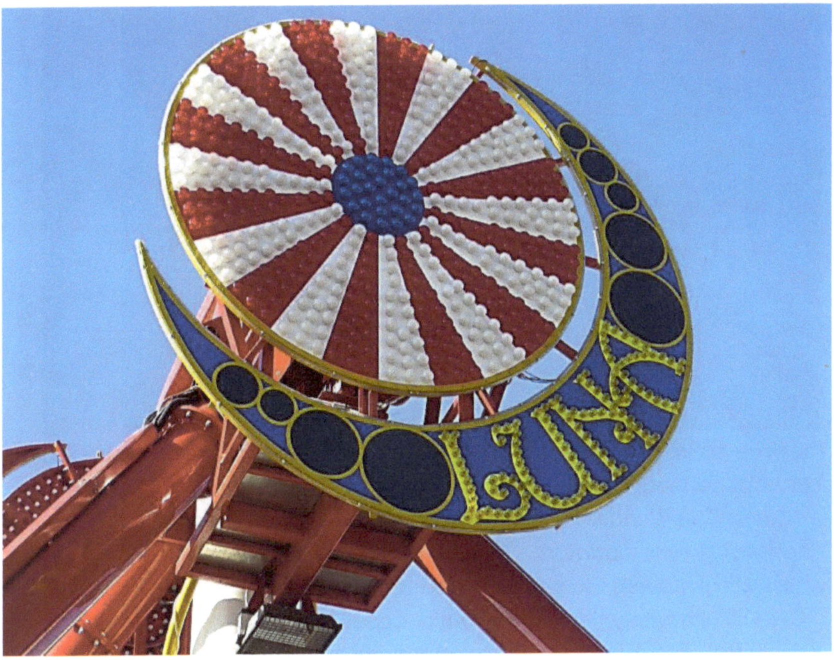

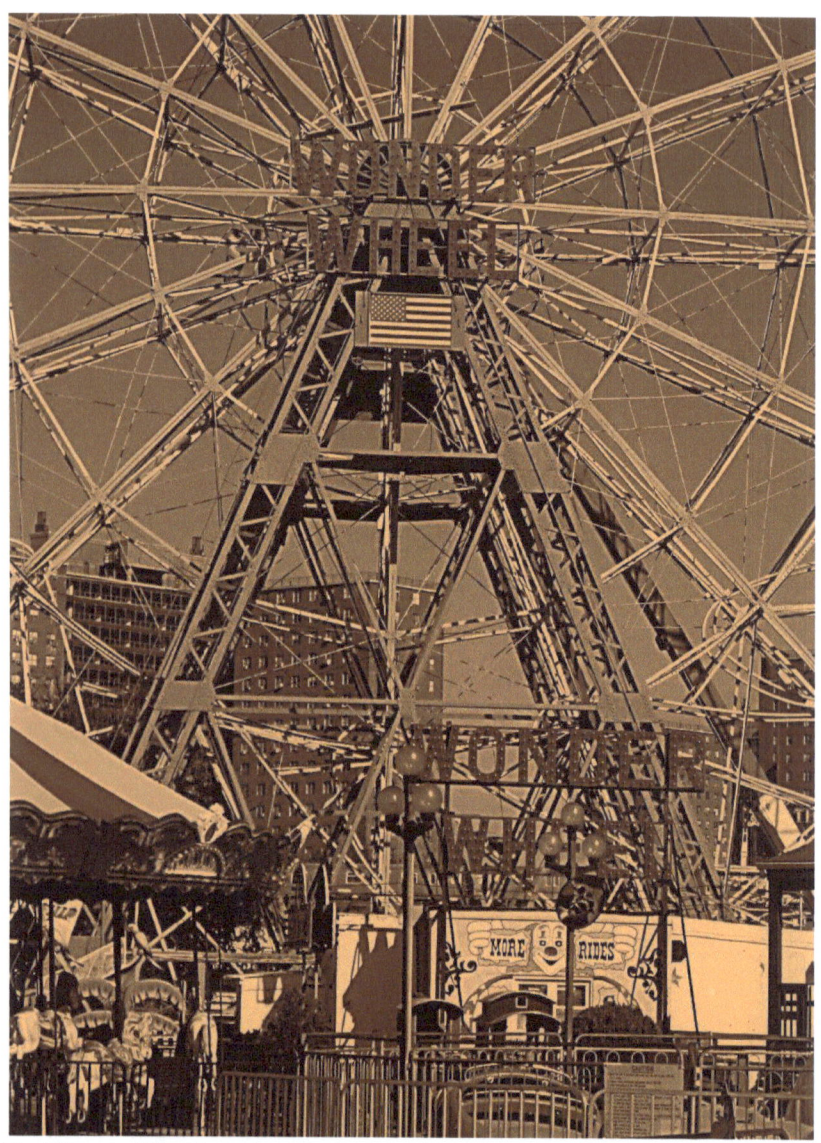

The Wonder Wheel was built in 1918 and opened in 1920, this steel Ferris wheel has both stationary cars and rocking cars that slide along a track. It holds 144 riders. The Wonder Wheel will remain thanks to laws protecting it as a national historic landmark. That is, unless CAI finds a loophole somewhere which will give them the power to decide a tragic fate. Changes proposed by CAI will ultimately destroy the soul of Coney Island. An area prized for its carney feel, side shows, and gritty atmosphere. Coney Island, surrounded by housing projects will become the new playground for New York's wealthy.

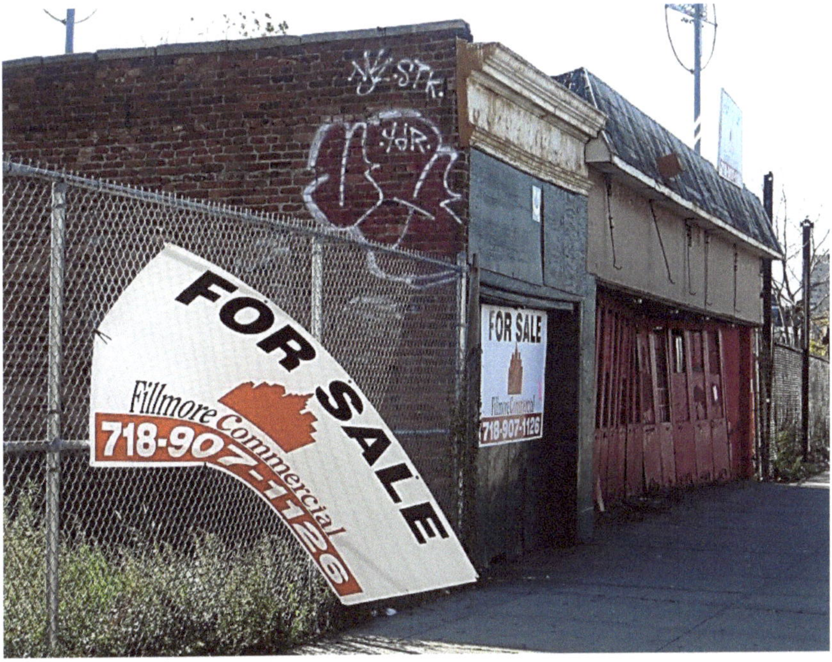
FOR SALE
Fillmore Commercial
718-907-1126
FOR SALE
Fillmore Commercial
718-907-1126

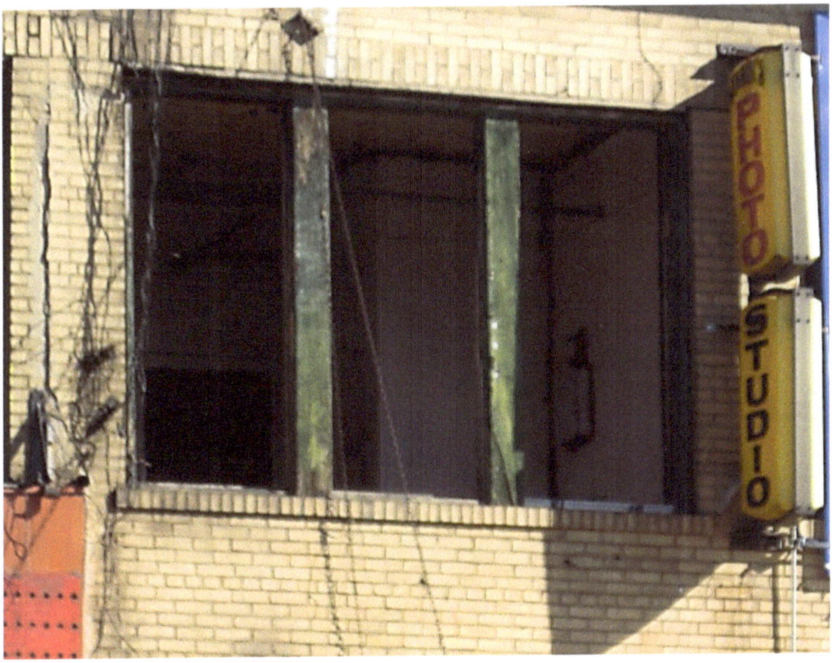
PHOTO
STUDIO

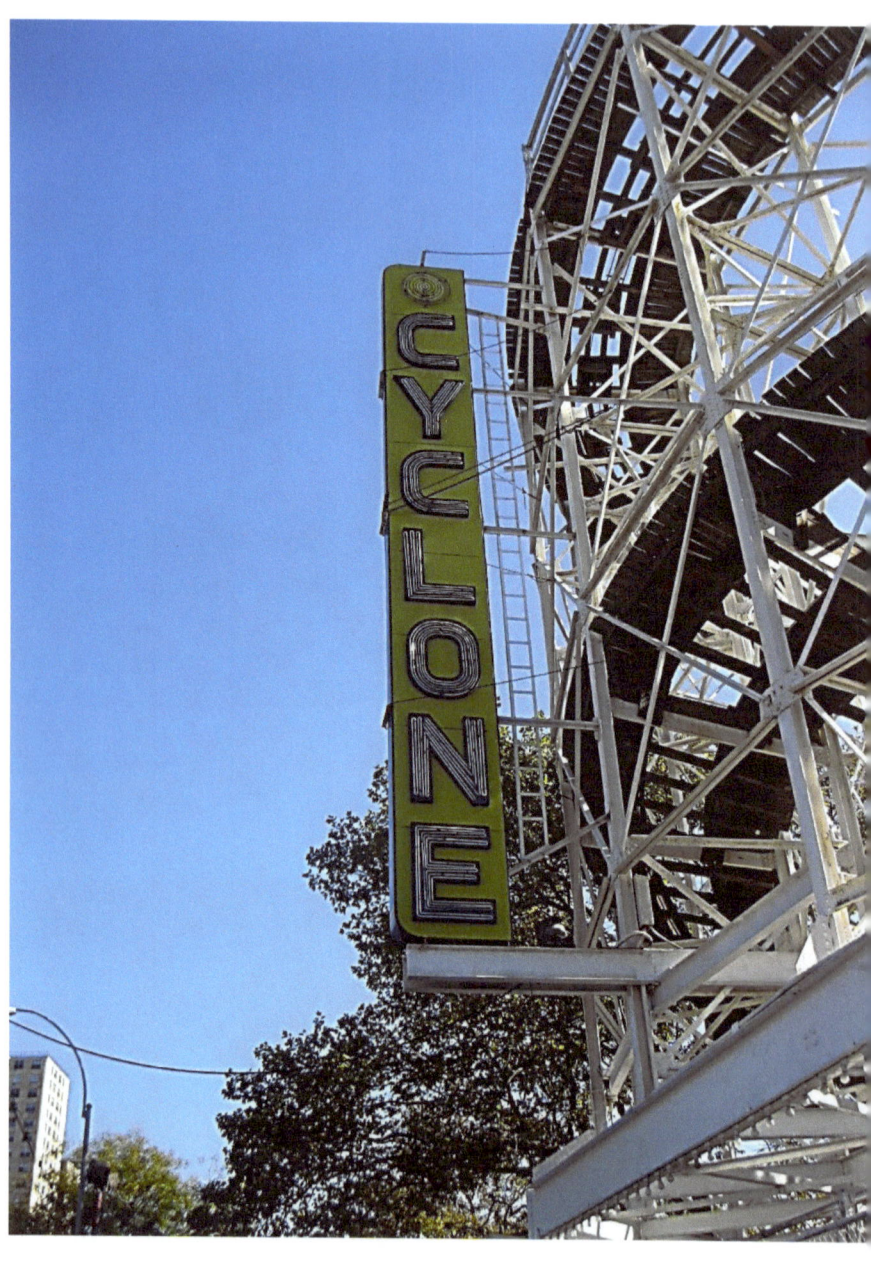

"Central Amusements International made and will continue to make its decisions regarding future occupants of the boardwalk based on who can best fulfill our vision" . . . . Valerio Ferrari, President

Sounds like an open invitation to Hard Rock and House of Blues !!

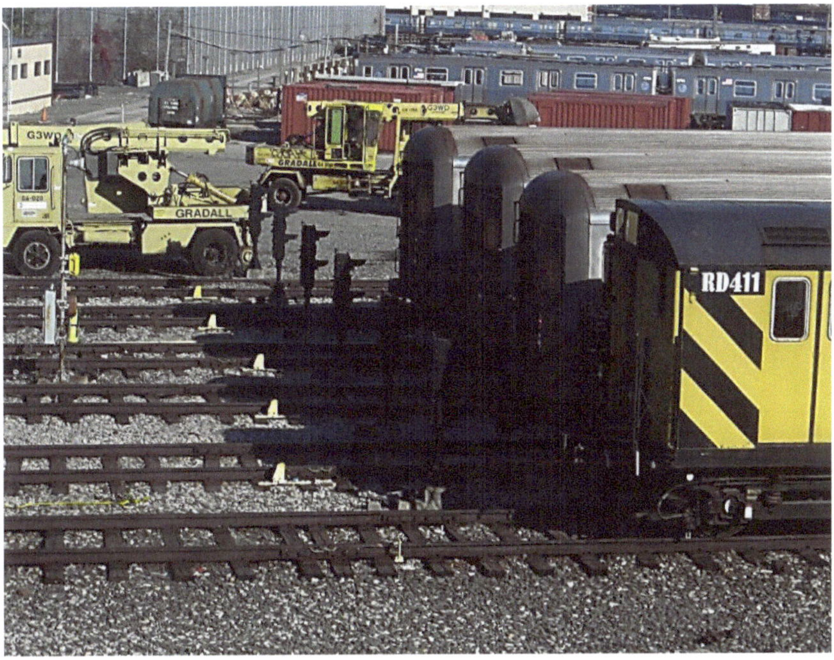
G3WD
GRADALL
RD411

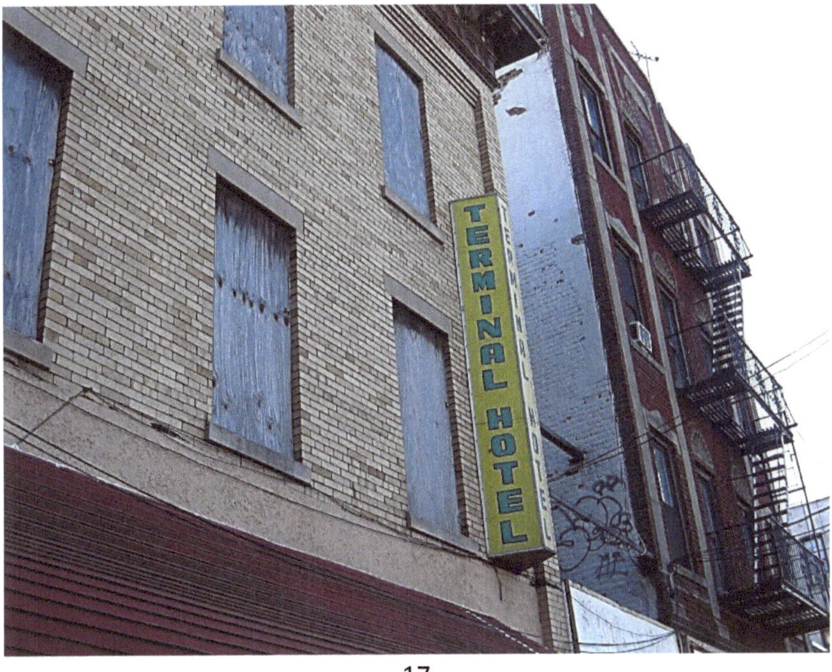
TERMINAL HOTEL

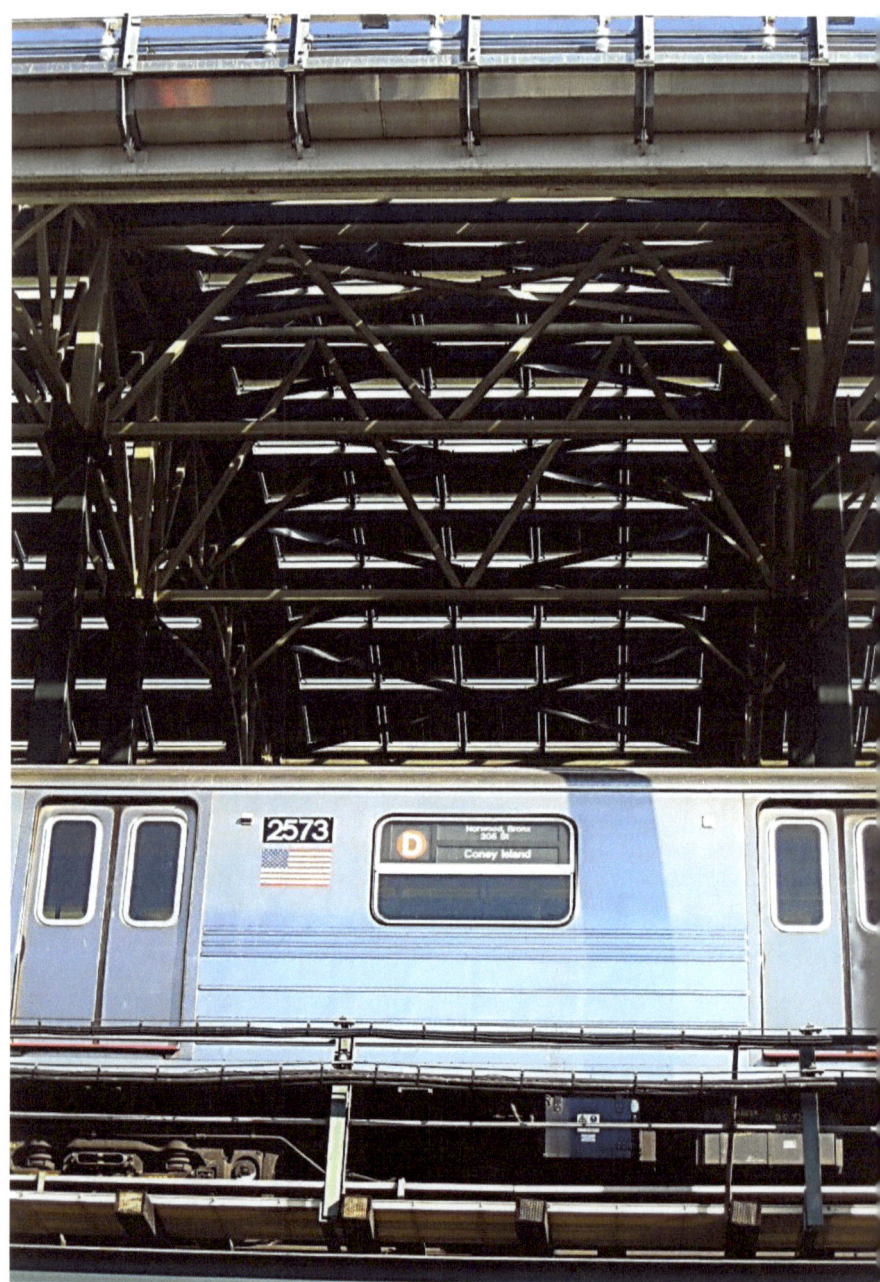

Several subway lines run directly into Coney Island, including D, N, and F lines. Coney Island features a two level elevated track at its station.

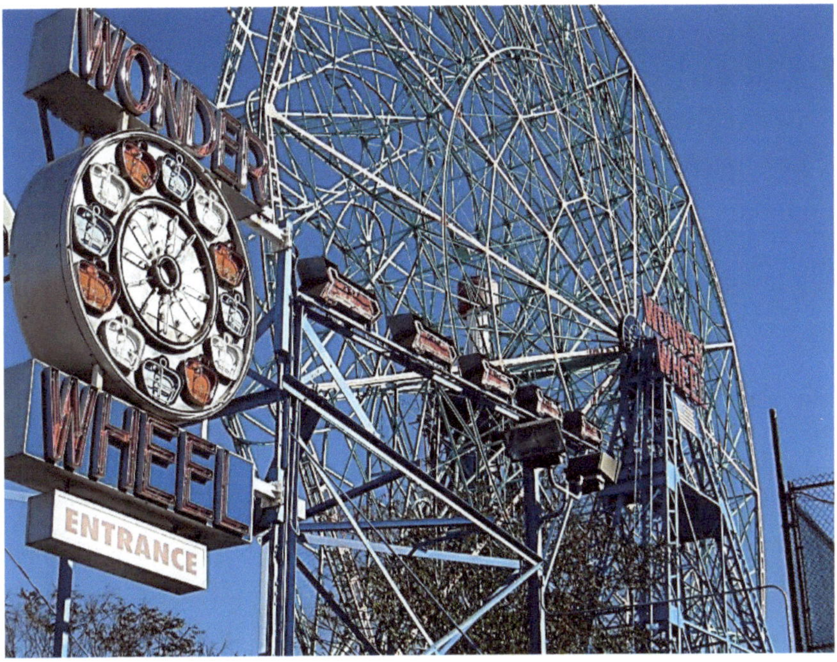
WONDER
WHEEL
ENTRANCE

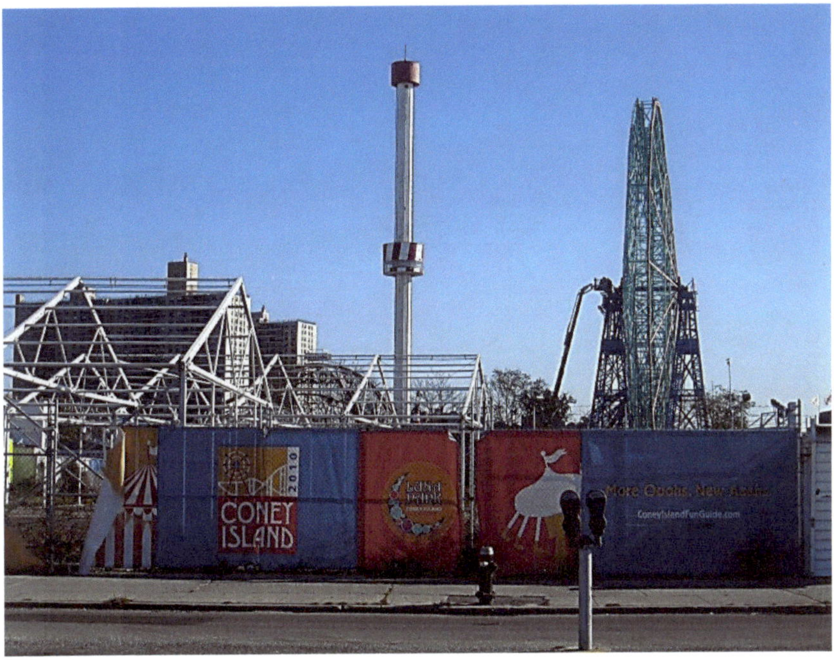
CONEY ISLAND
2010

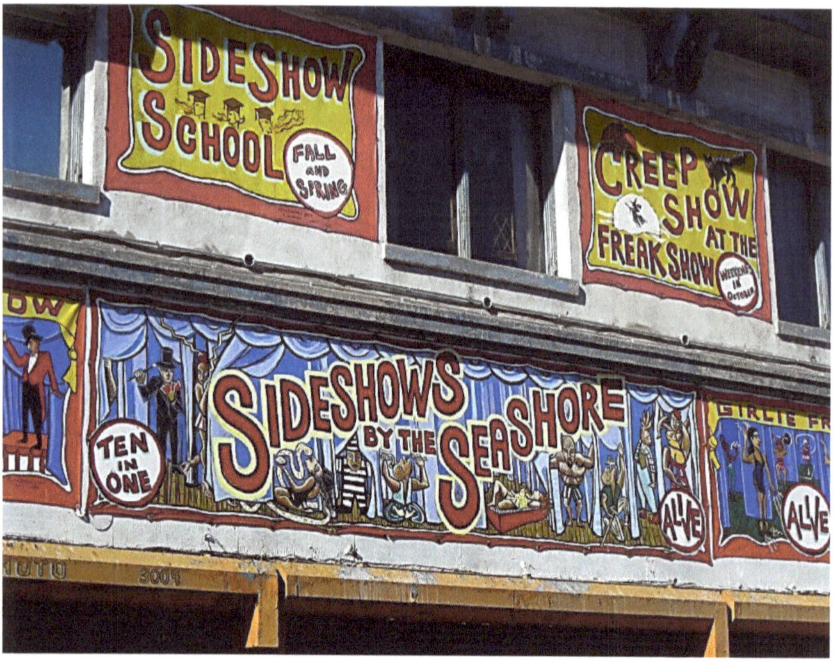
SIDESHOW SCHOOL
FALL AND SPRING
CREEP SHOW AT THE FREAK SHOW
SIDESHOWS BY THE SEASHORE
TEN IN ONE
ALIVE
ALIVE

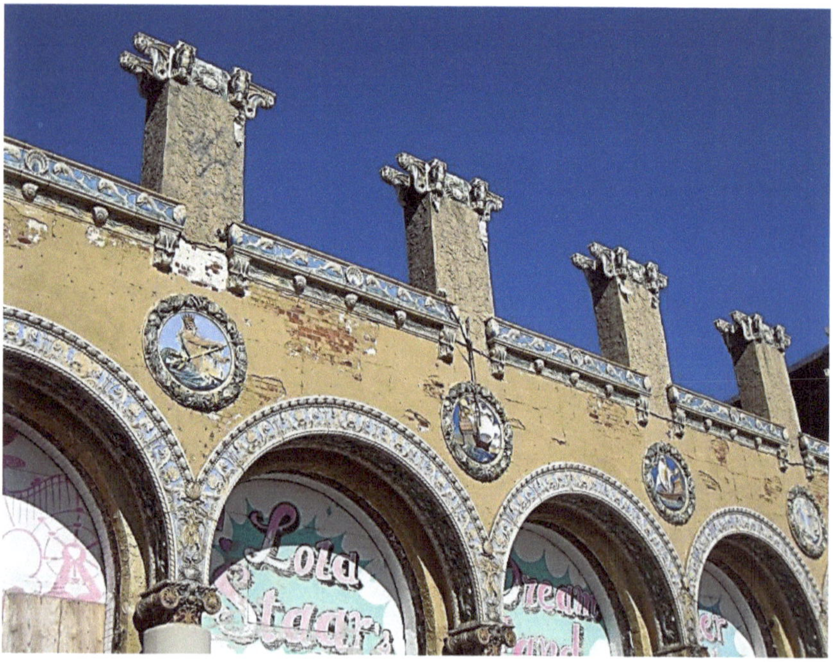
Lola

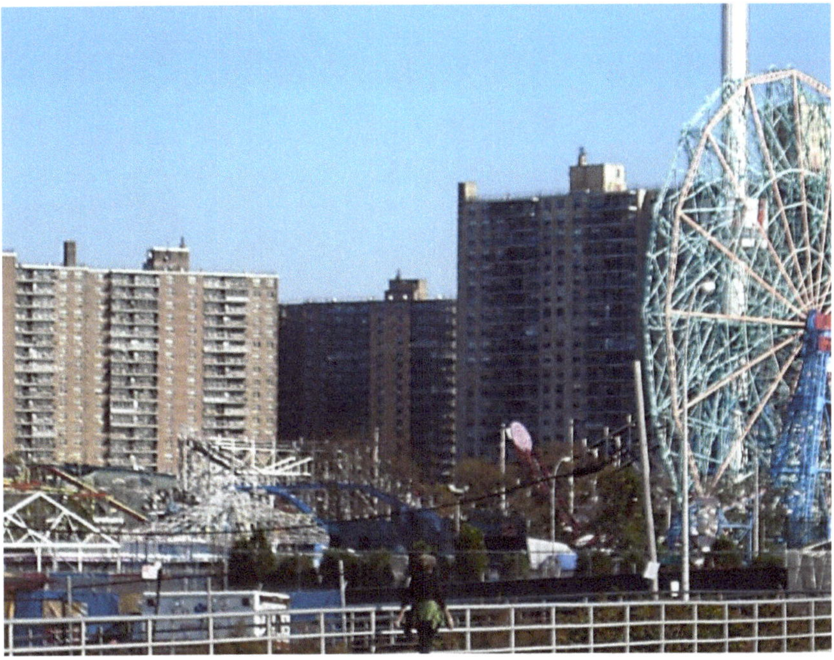

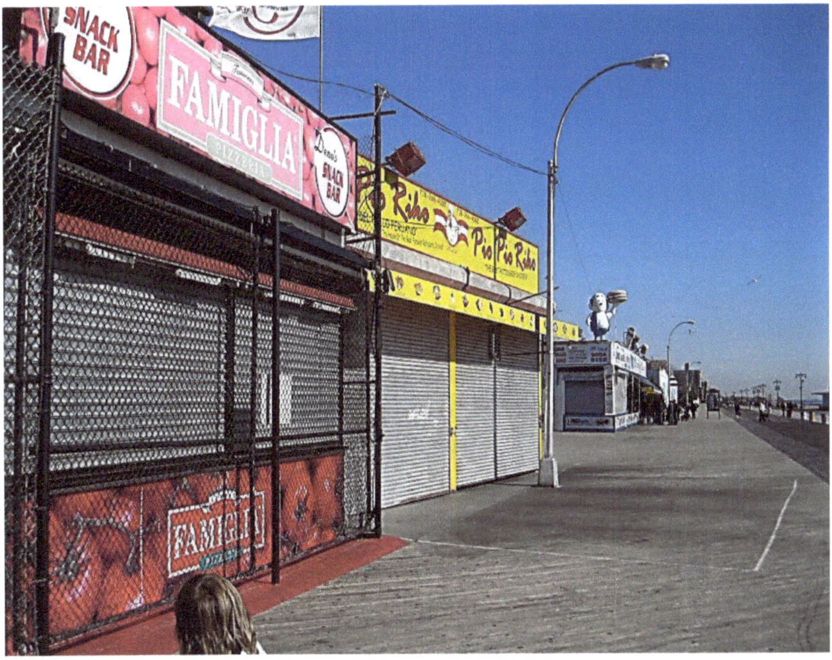
SNACK BAR
FAMIGLIA
SNACK BAR
Pio Pio Riko
FAMIGLIA

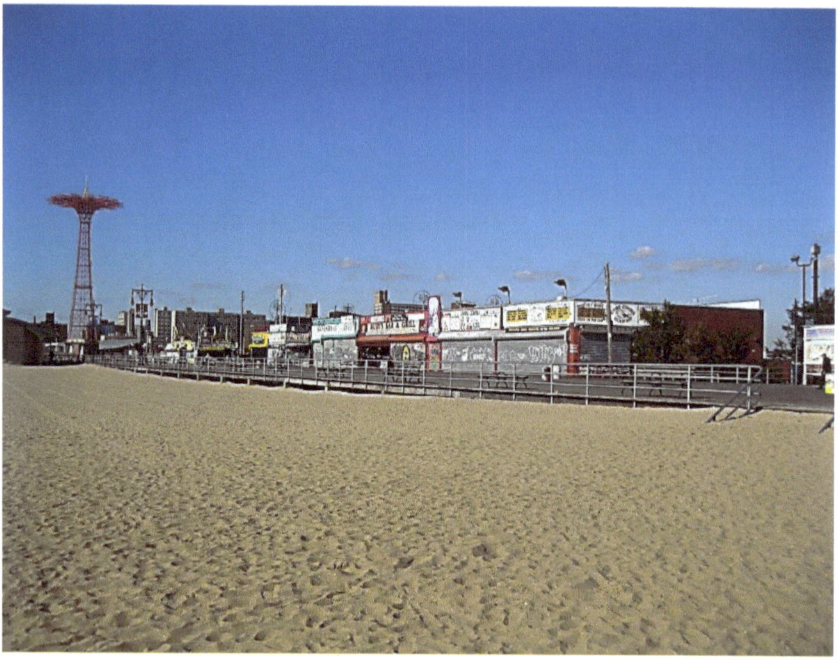

Sadly Coney Islands beaches are dirty and full of broken glass practically everywhere you look. Watch out for that occasional hypodermic.

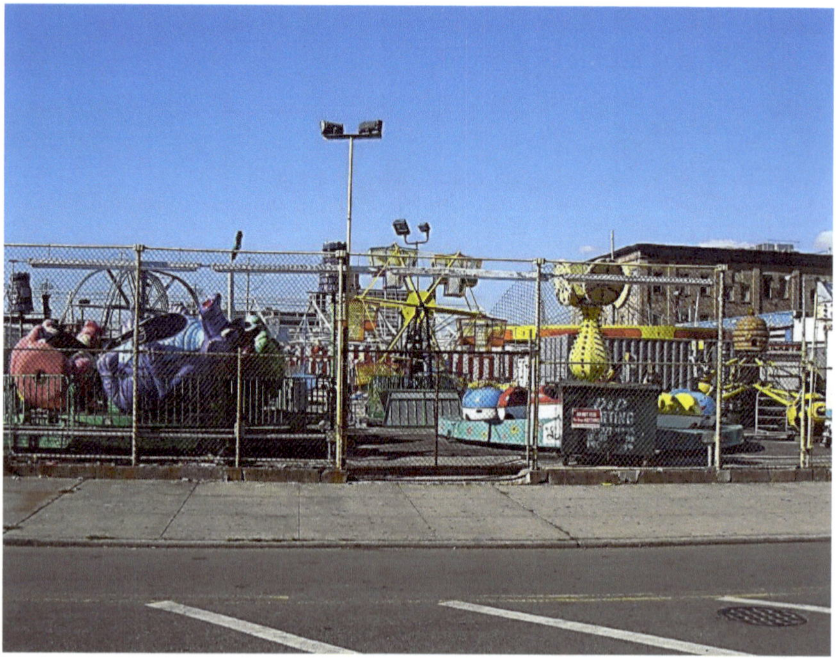

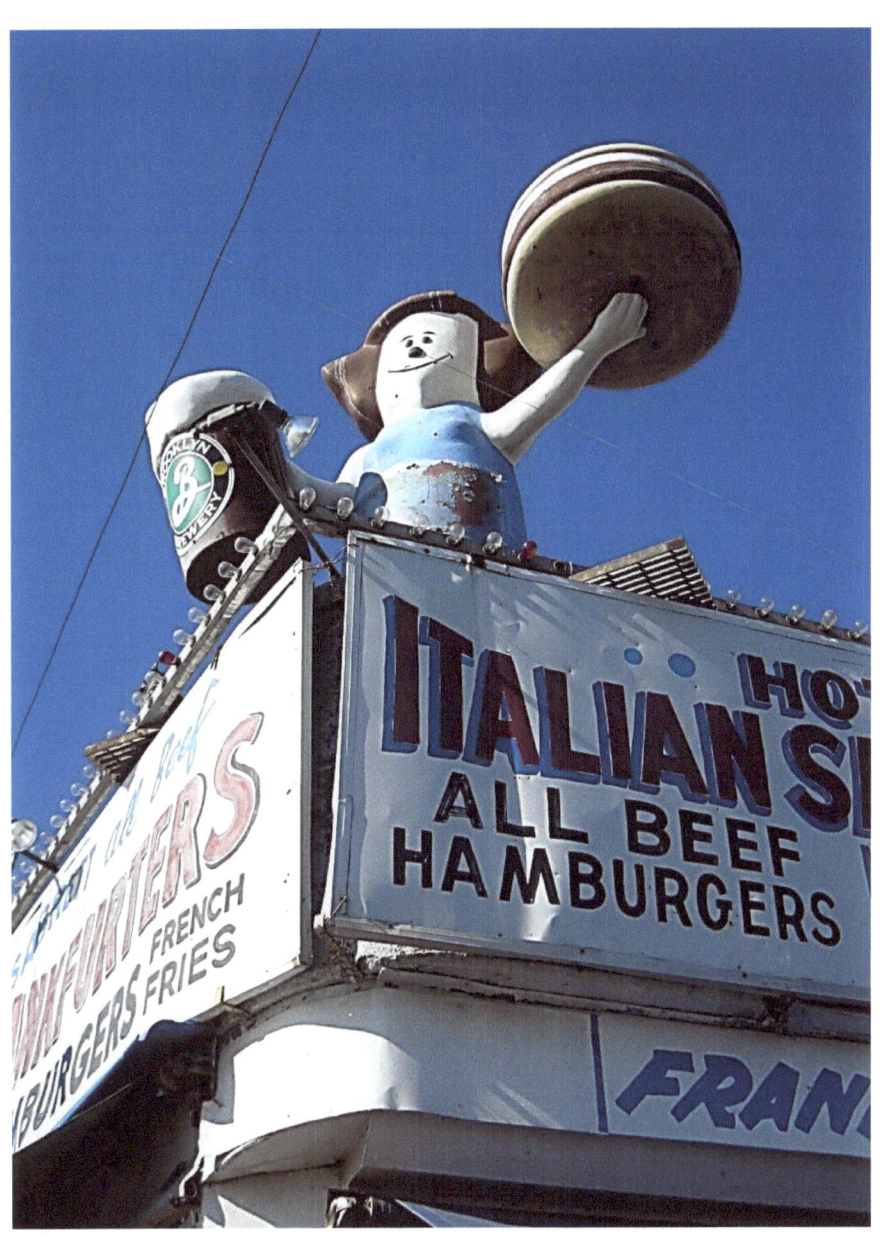

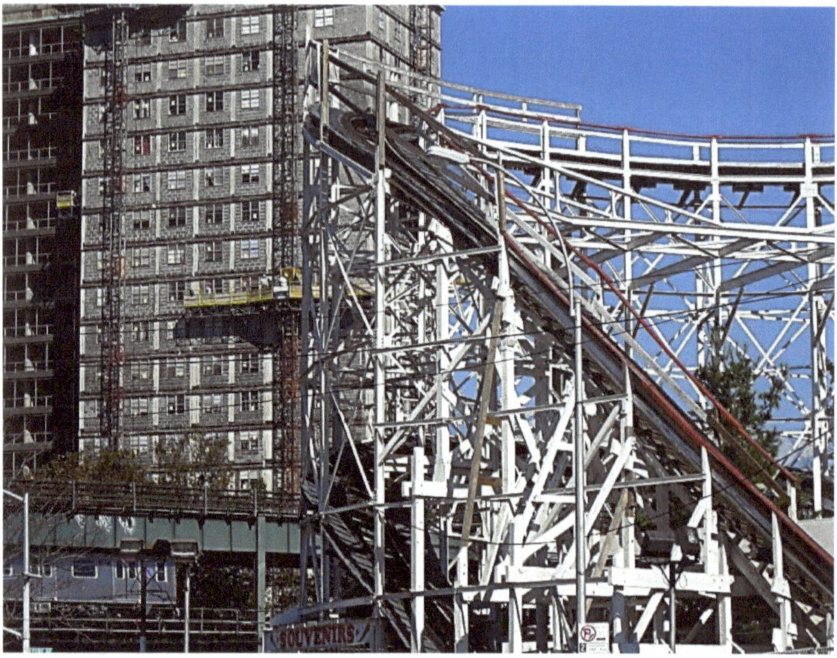
SOUVENIRS

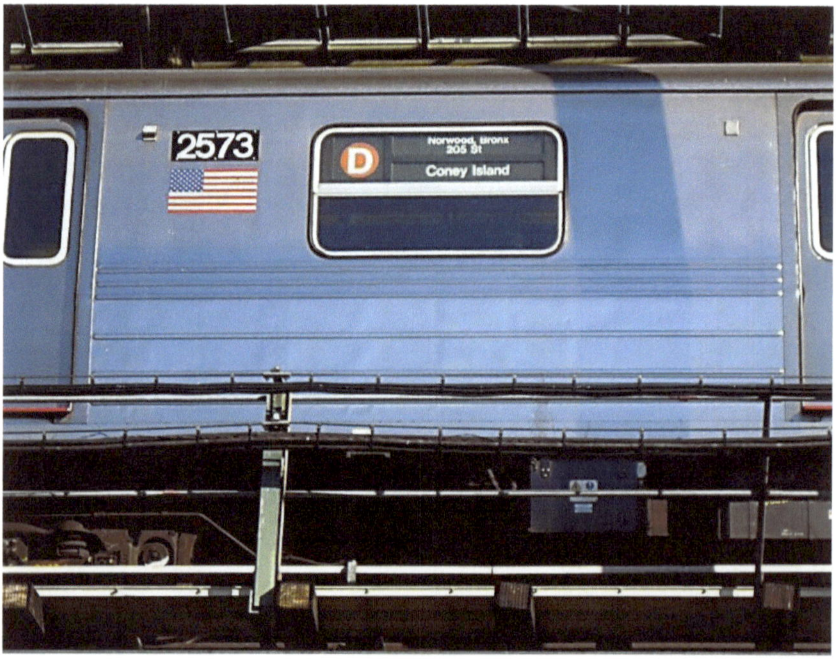
2573
D
Norwood, Bronx
205 St
Coney Island

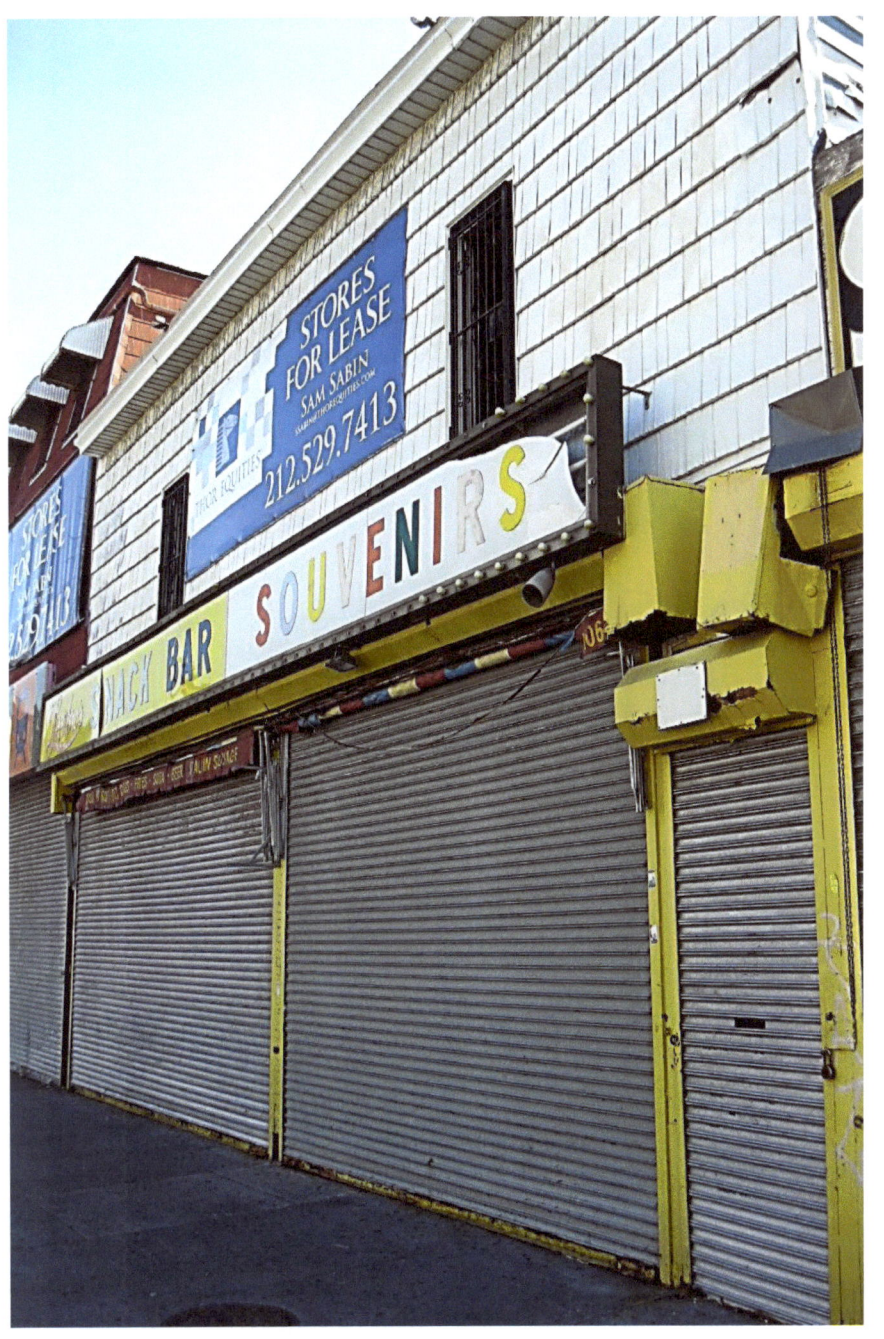

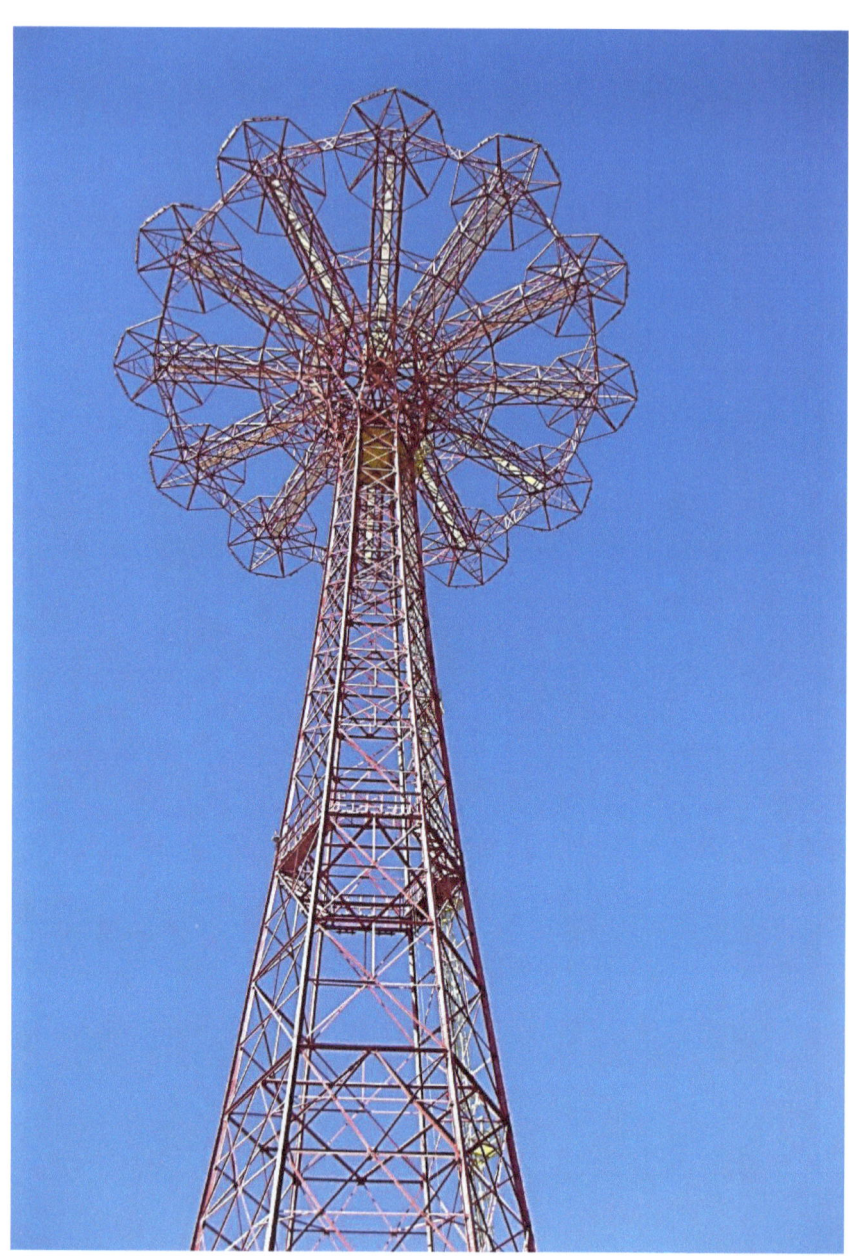

The long abandoned parachute drop, now just a skeleton, originally the Life Savers Parachute Jump at the 1939 New York World's Fair, was the first ride of its kind. Patrons were hoisted 190 feet in the air before being allowed to drop using guy-wired parachutes. Although the ride has been closed since 1968, it remains a Coney Island landmark.

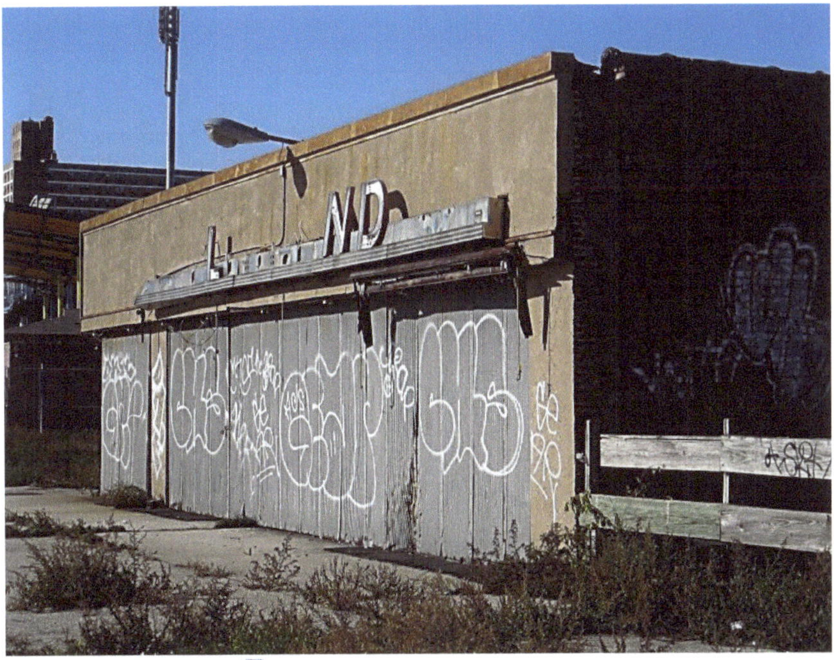

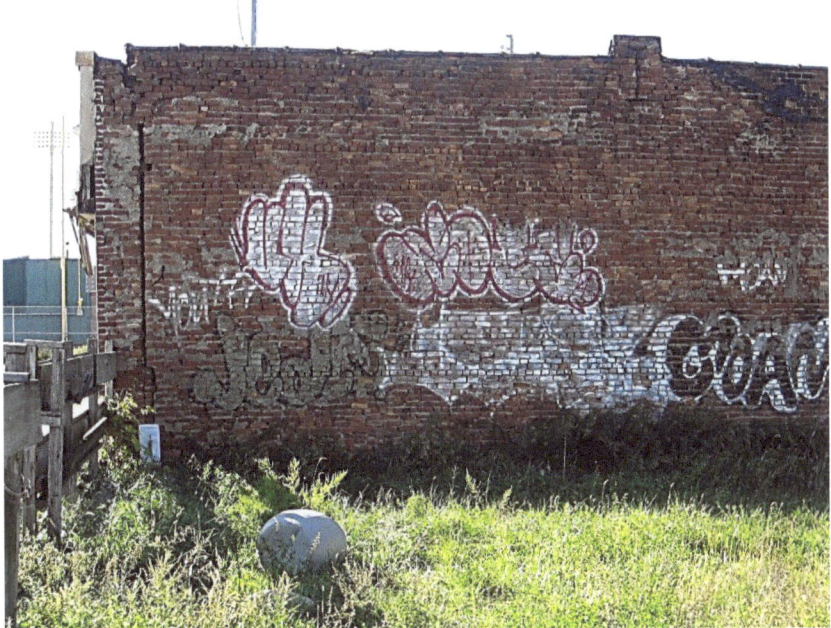

Boarded up and run down buildings are abundant all over Coney Island and the boardwalk.

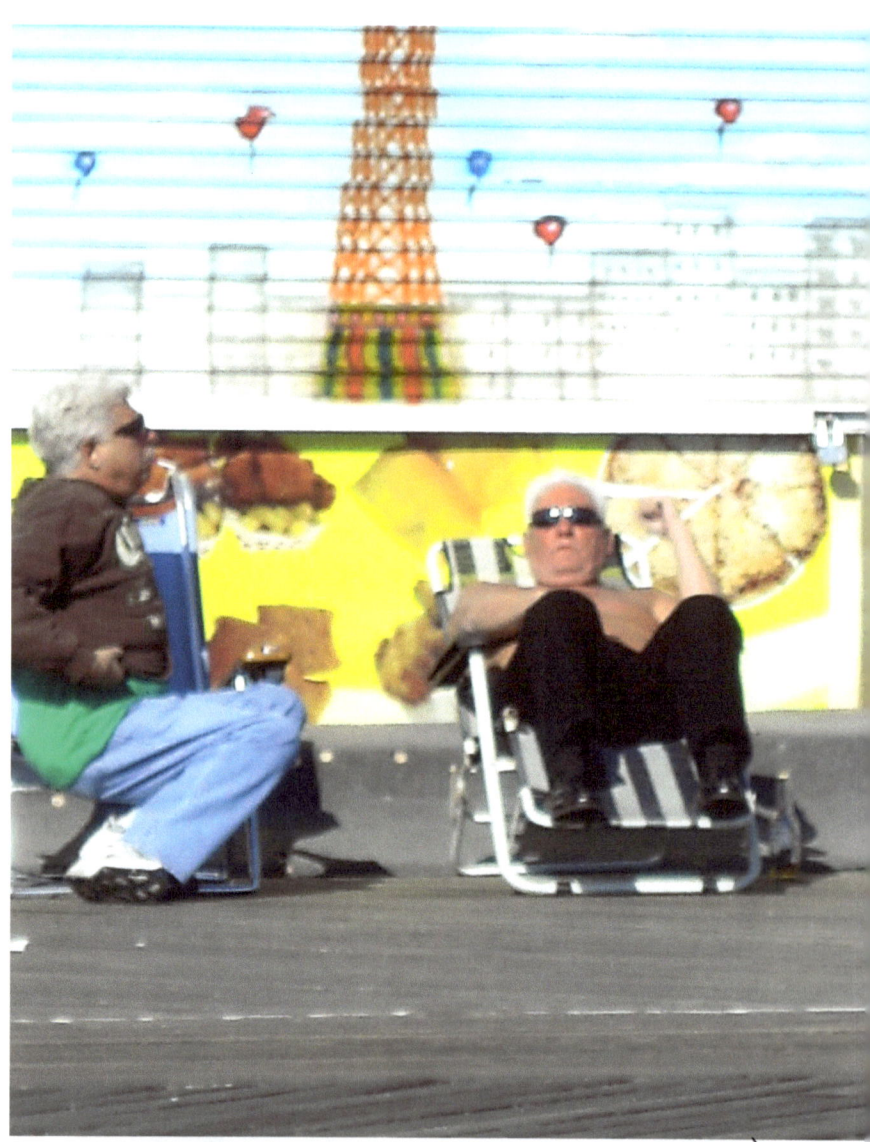

People from all walks make up the colorful and interesting mix of people who frequent the boardwalk. Once Central Amusements does there thing, these die-hard New Yorker's and other people will be a vision from the past.

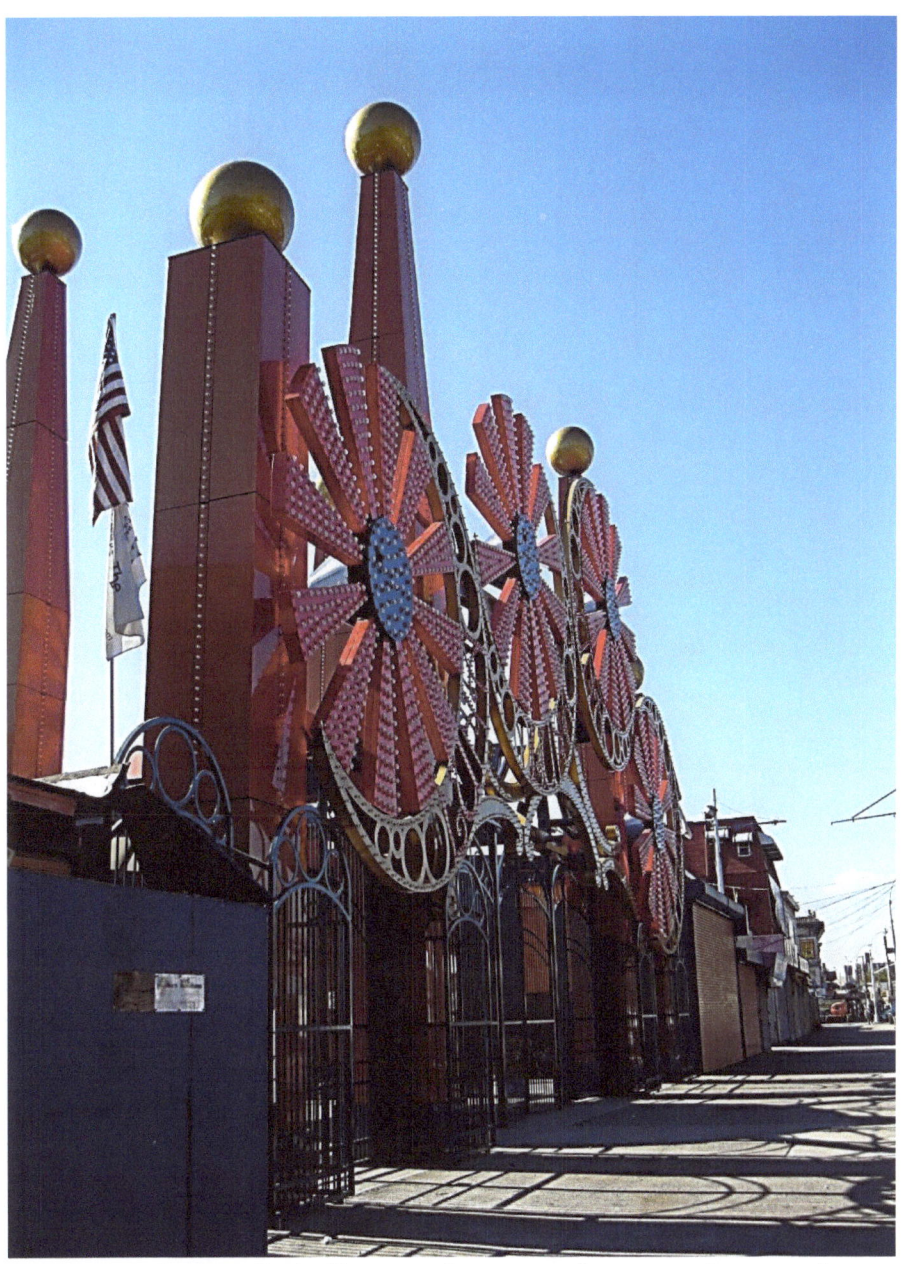

The modern day Luna Park. The original was opened in 1903 and continued to operate until it closed in 1946. The original park featured 250,000 lights which made for an incredible sight during that time period.

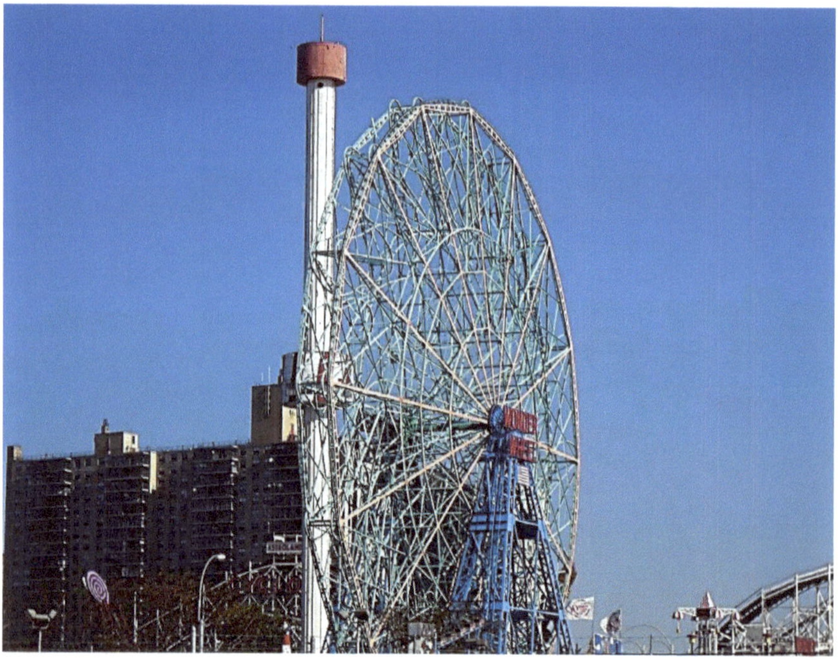

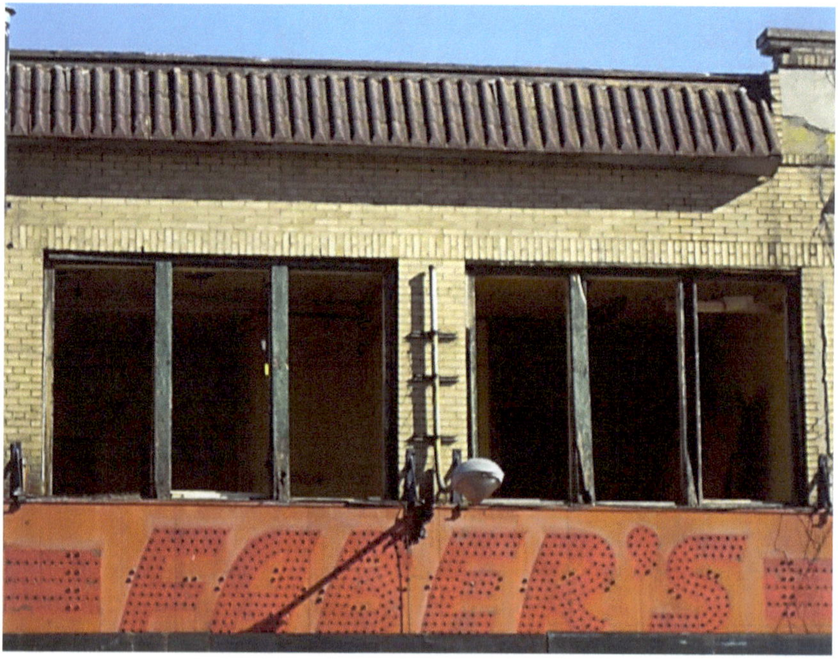

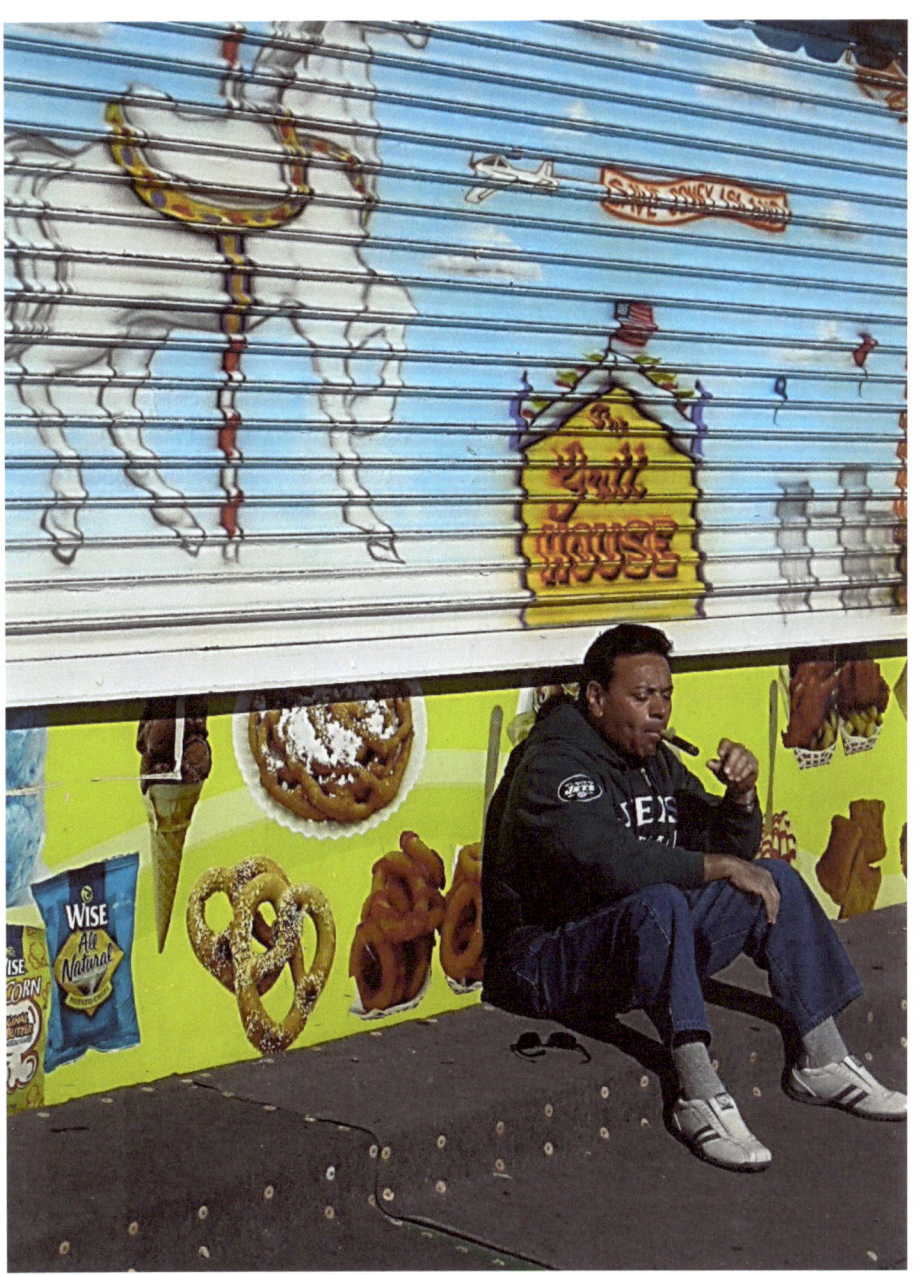

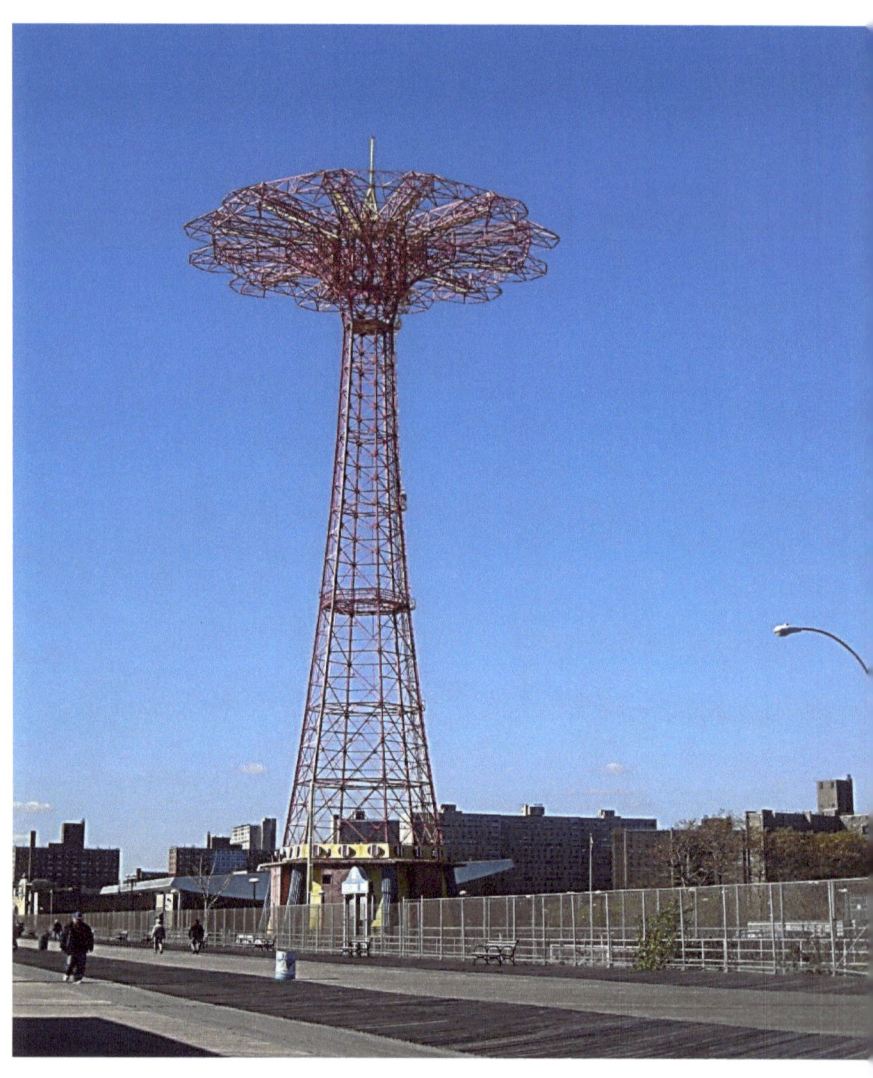

The B&B Carousel was Coney Island's last traditional carousel. It is now surrounded by furniture stores, near the old entrance to Luna Park. When the long-term operator died unexpectedly, the carousel was put up for auction, and it was feared the ride would leave Coney Island or would be broken up for sale to collectors, being one of the last intact traditional carousels in the U.S. still in private hands. The City of New York bought the Carousel a few days before the auction. It has been dismantled and will operate in Coney Island; the specific location is still to be determined. That now may never happen.

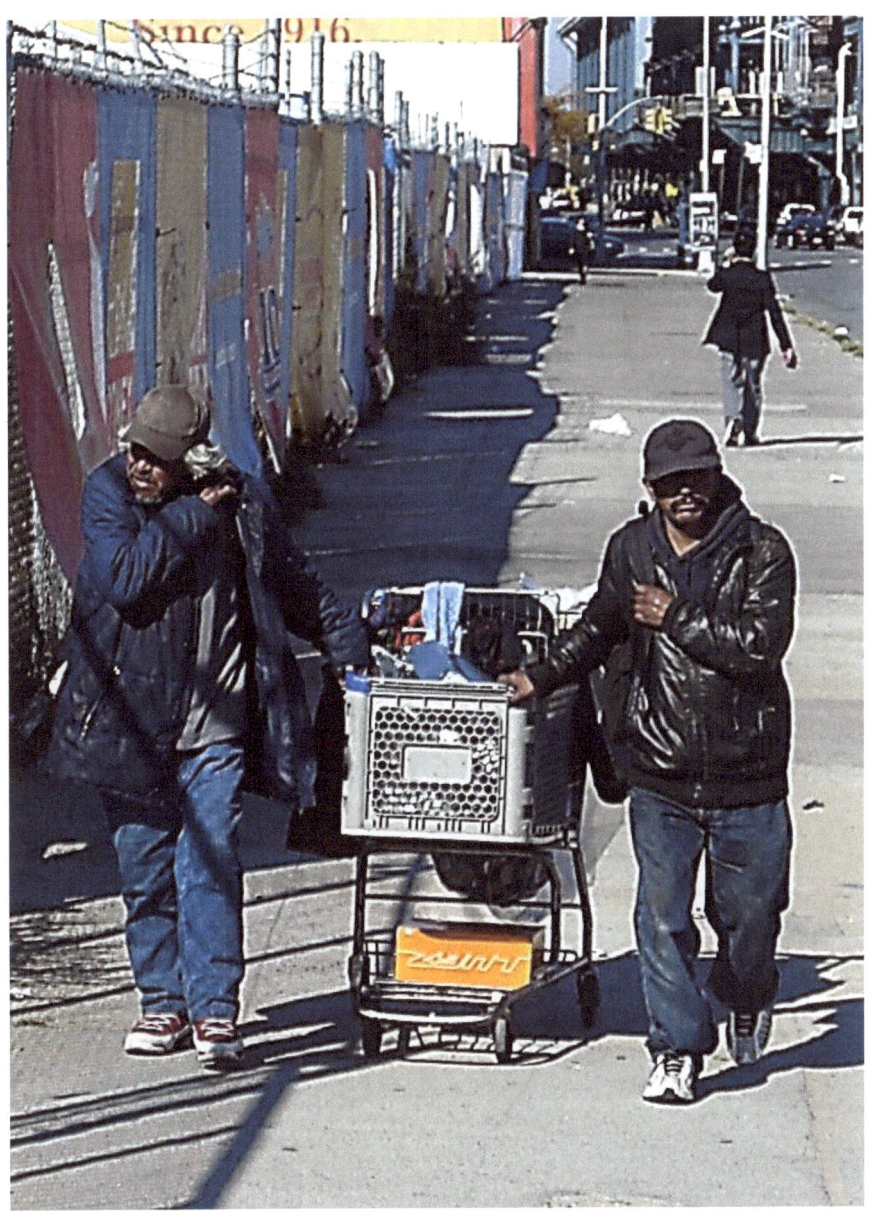

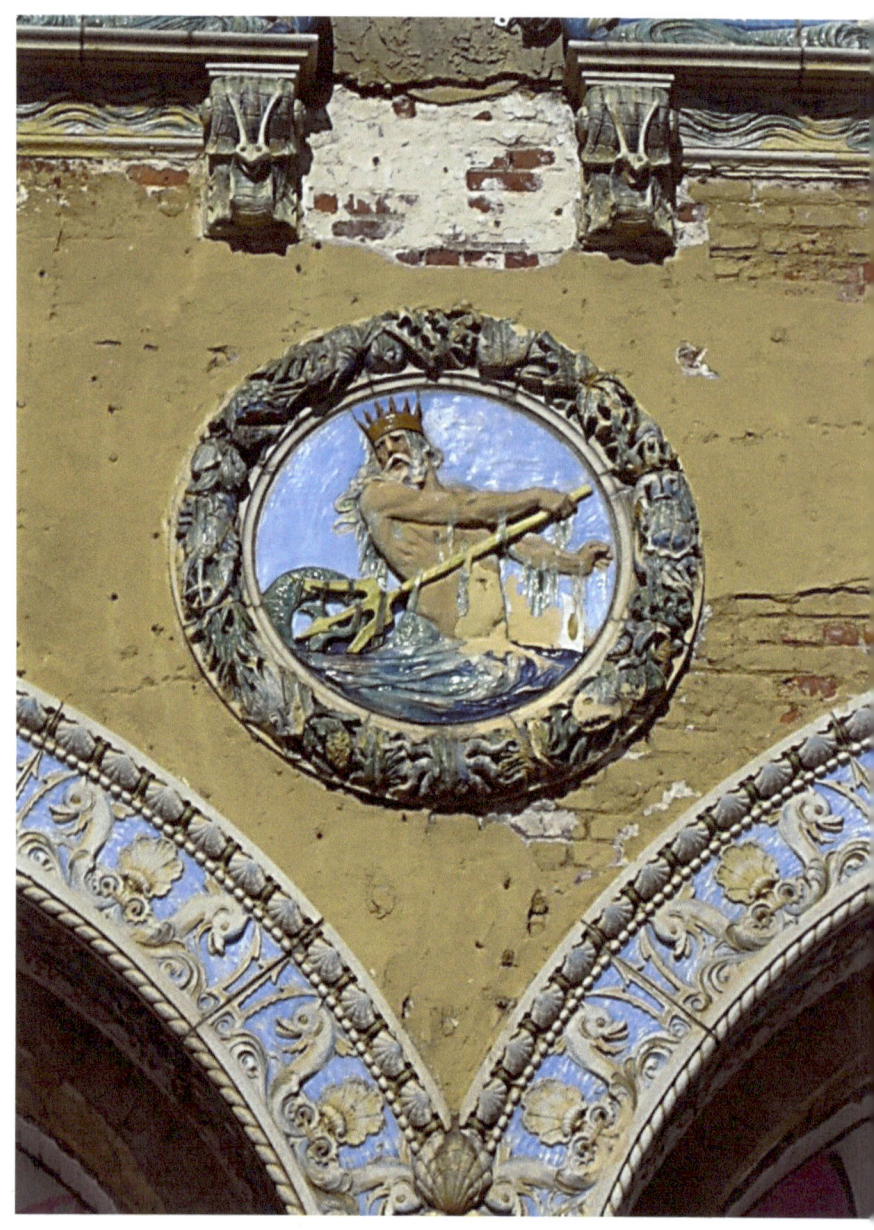

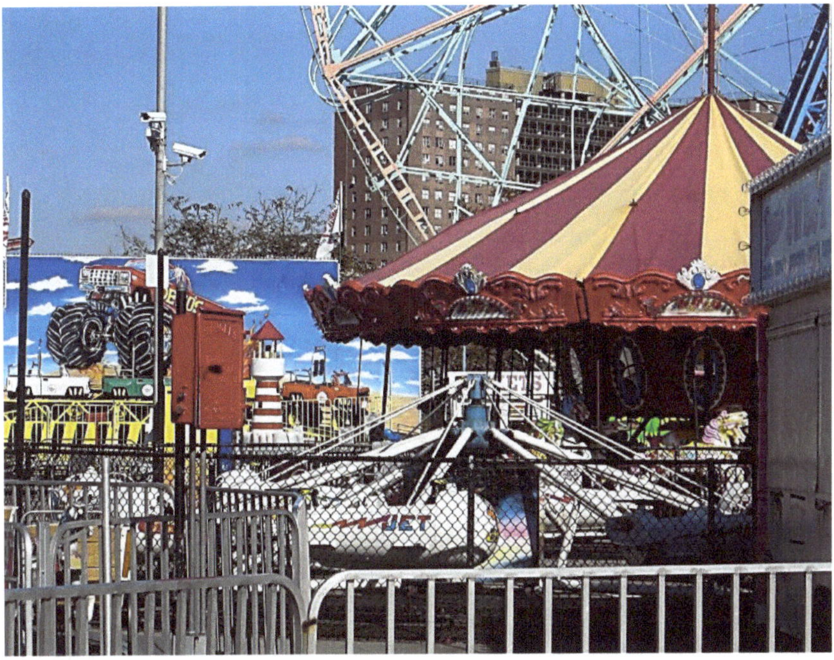

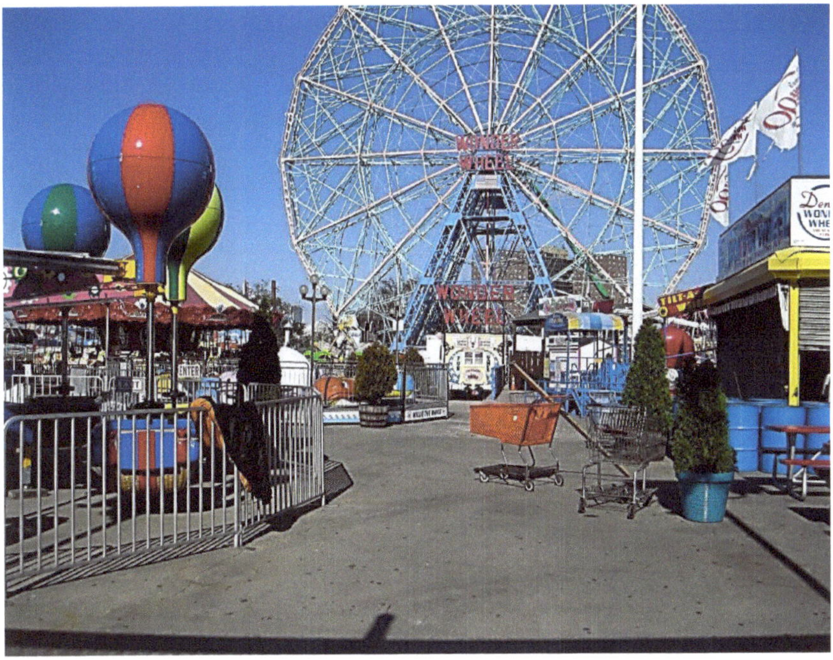

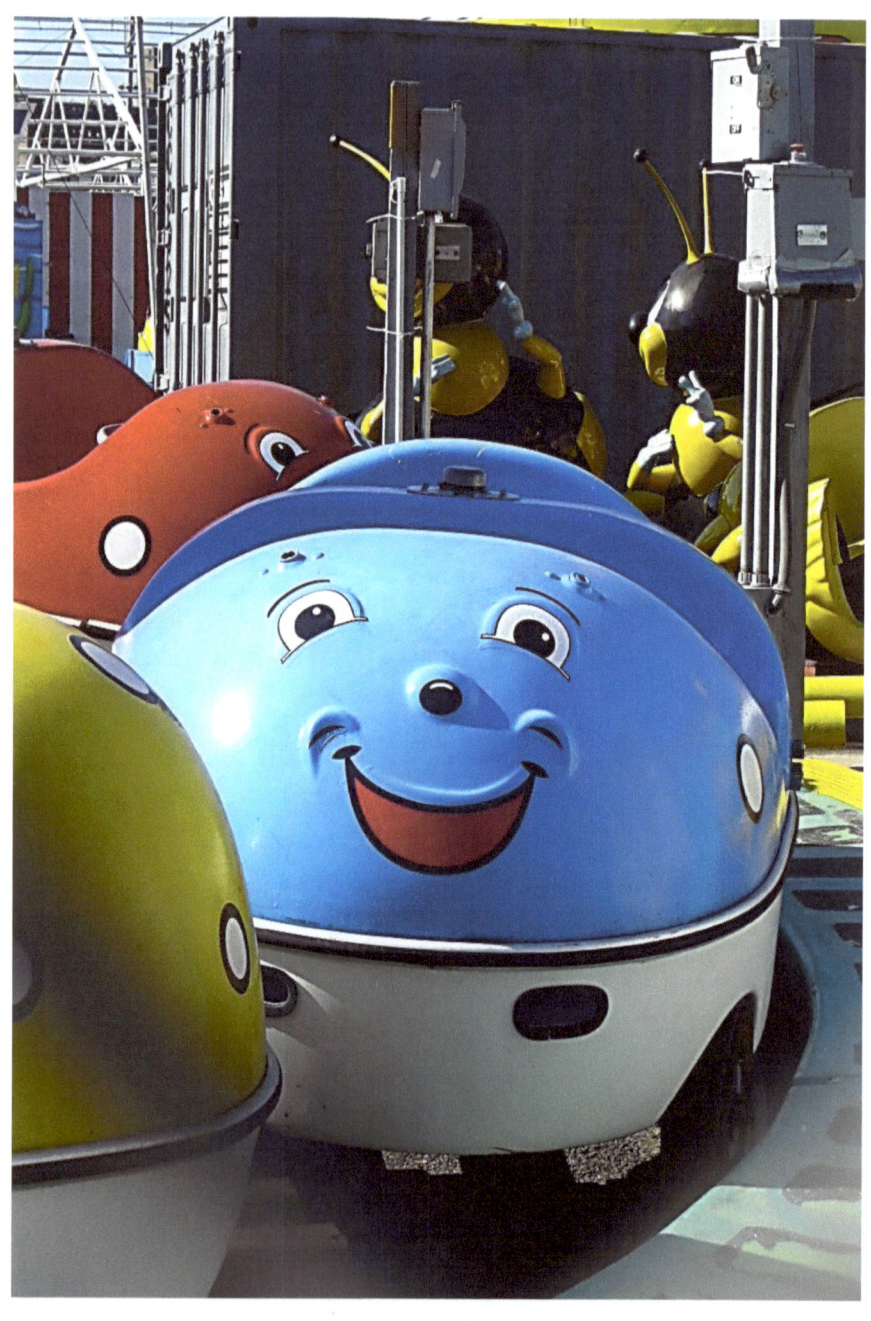

Several of the music scenes for the Banana Splits TV show were actually filmed in Coney Island.

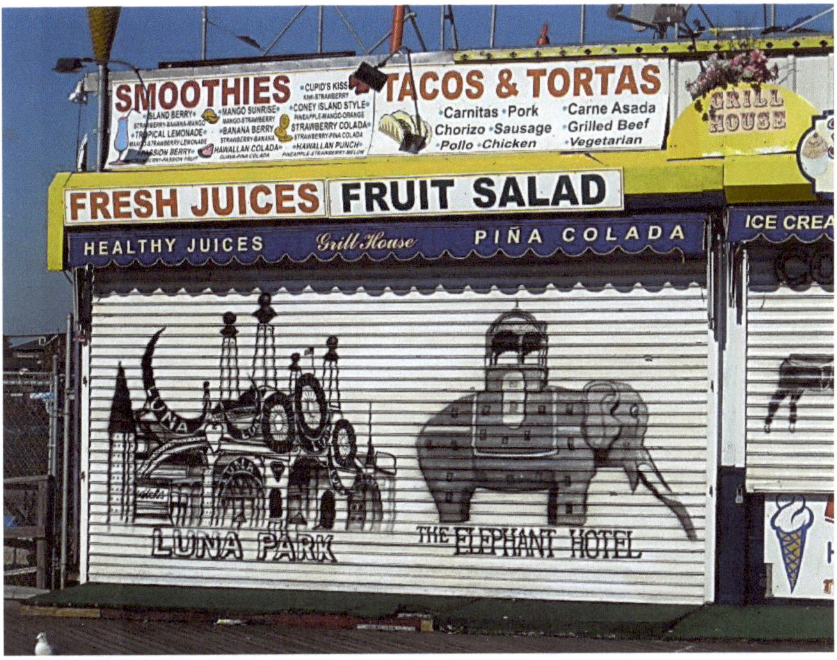
SMOOTHIES
TACOS & TORTAS
•Carnitas •Pork
•Carne Asada
Chorizo •Sausage
•Grilled Beef
•Pollo •Chicken
•Vegetarian
GRILL HOUSE
FRESH JUICES
FRUIT SALAD
HEALTHY JUICES
Grill House
PIÑA COLADA
LUNA PARK
THE ELEPHANT HOTEL

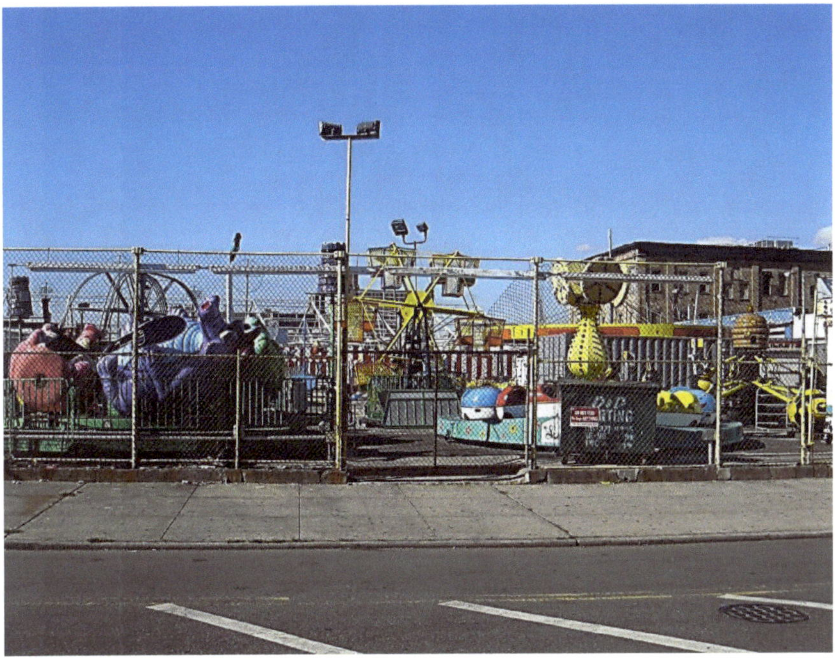

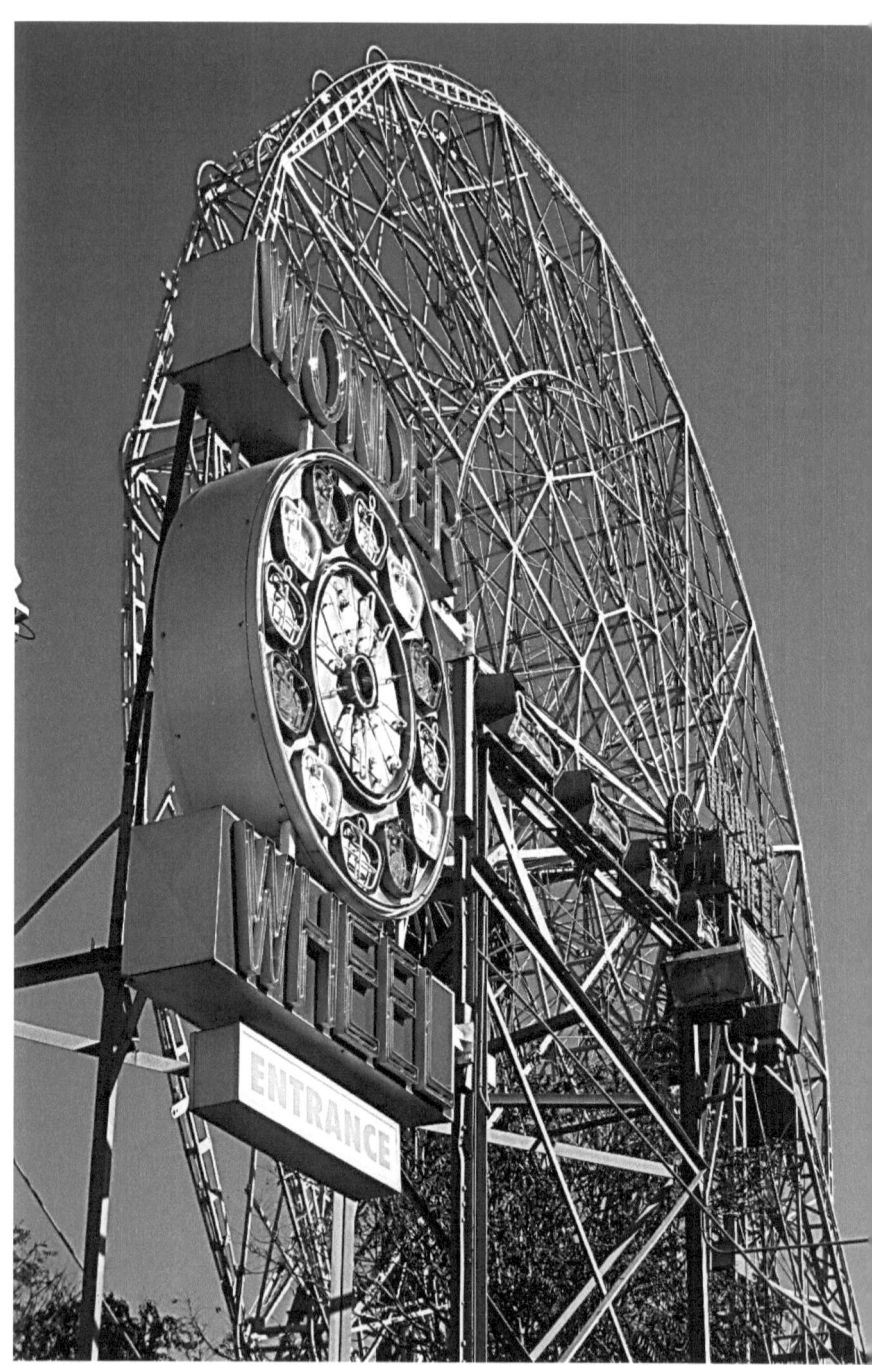

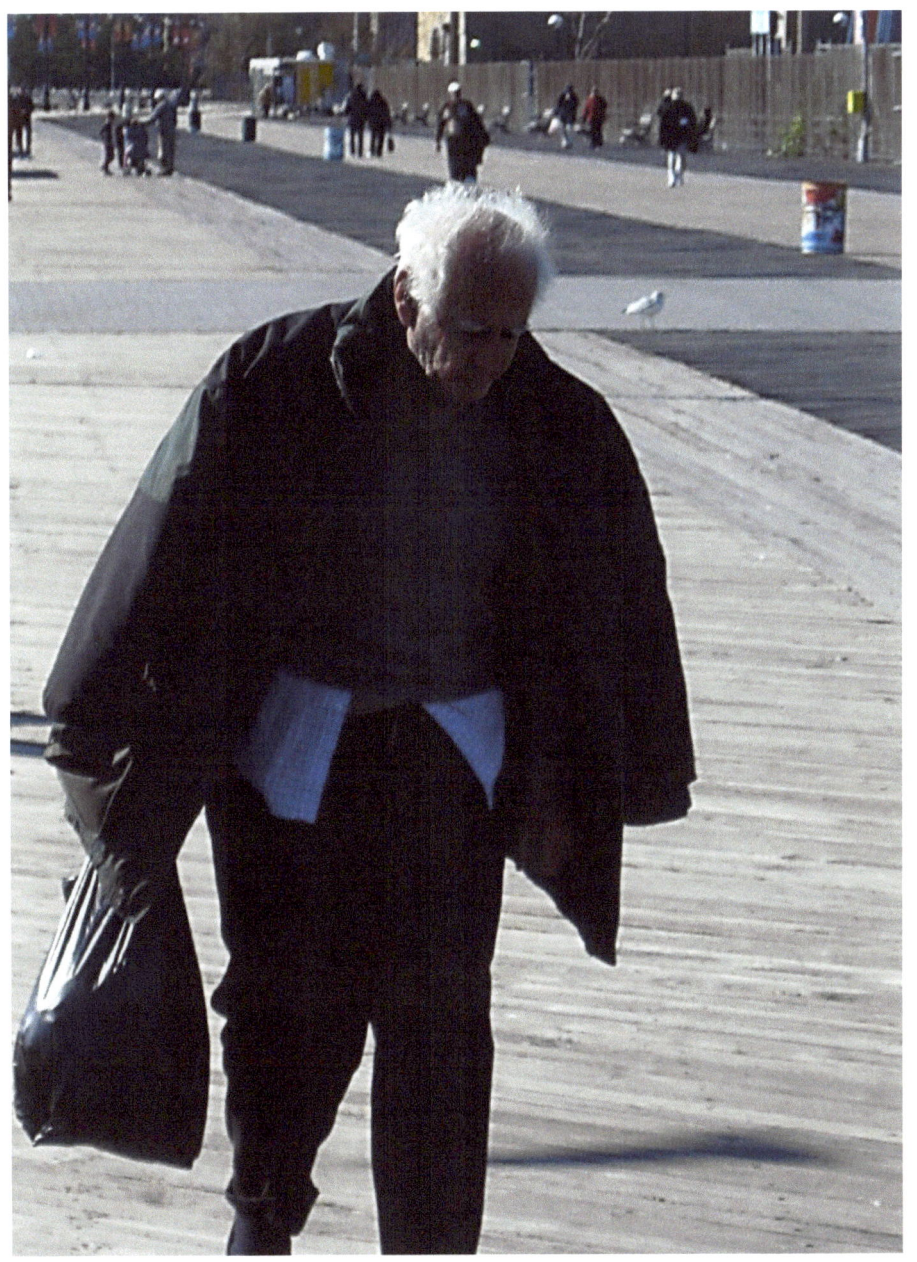

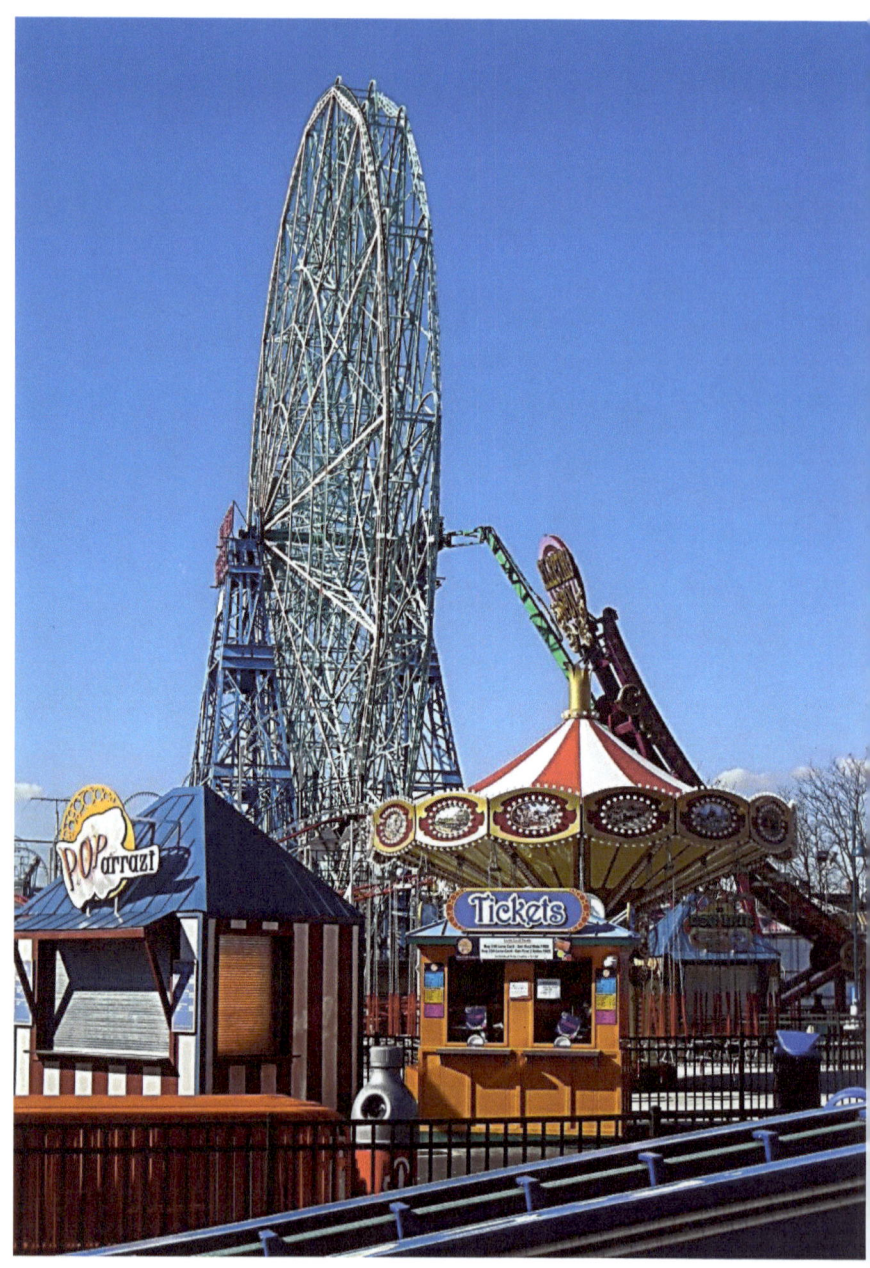

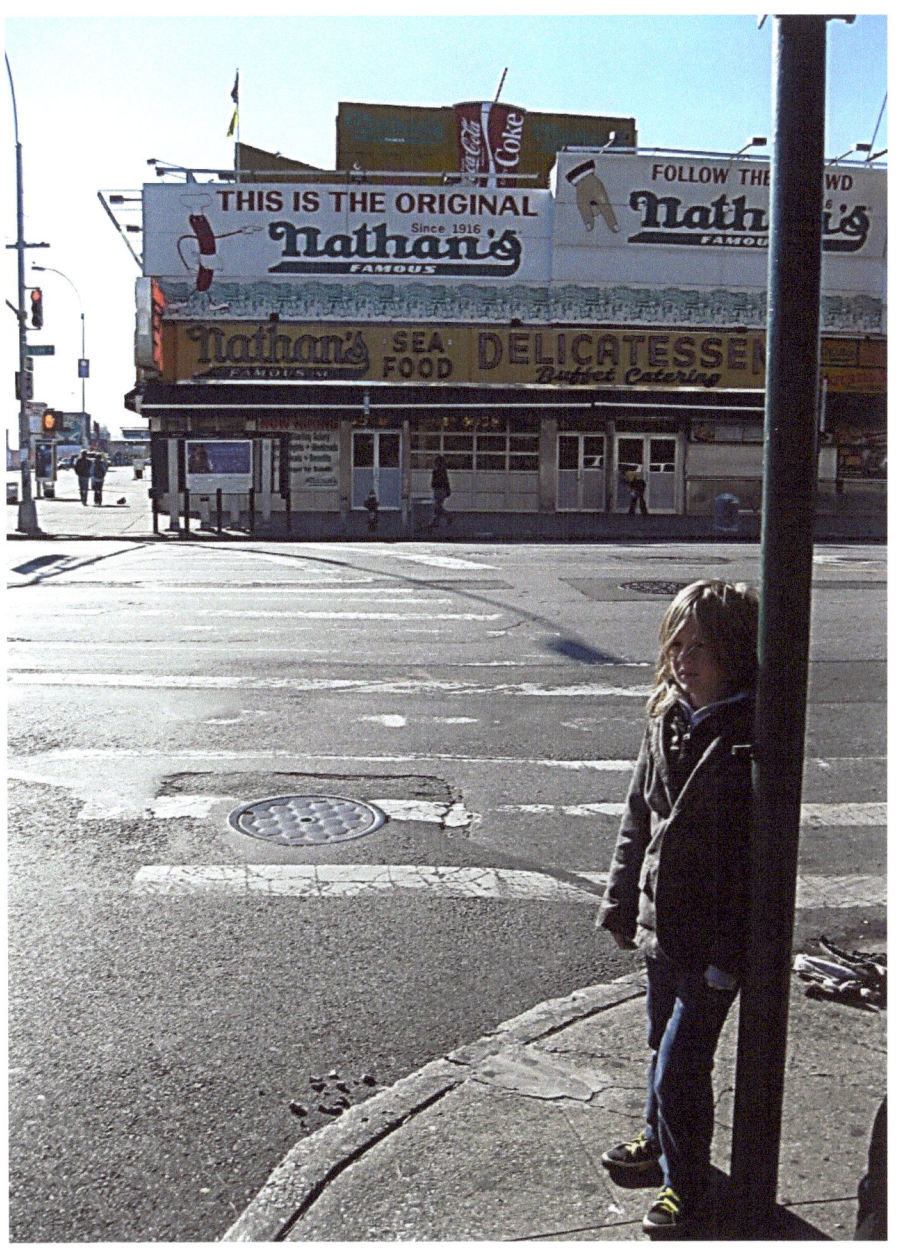

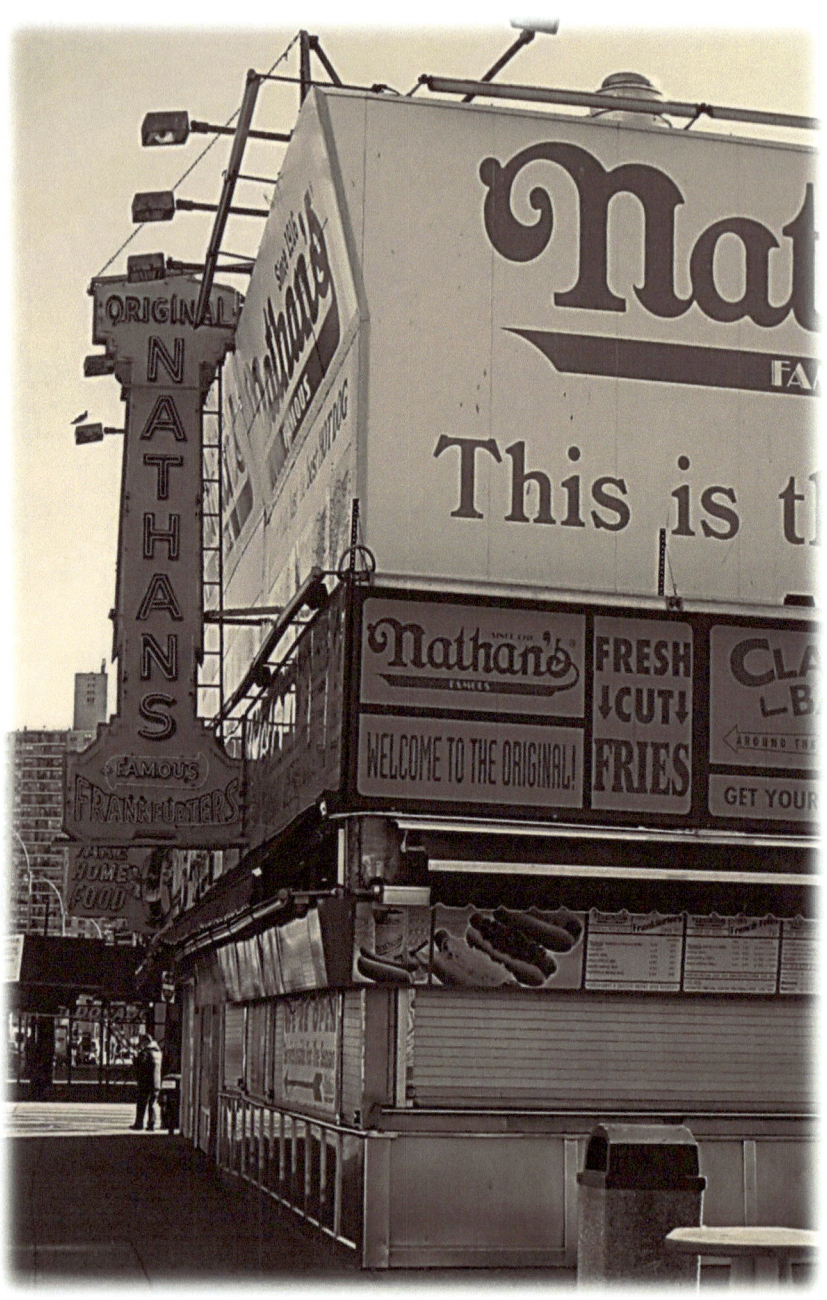

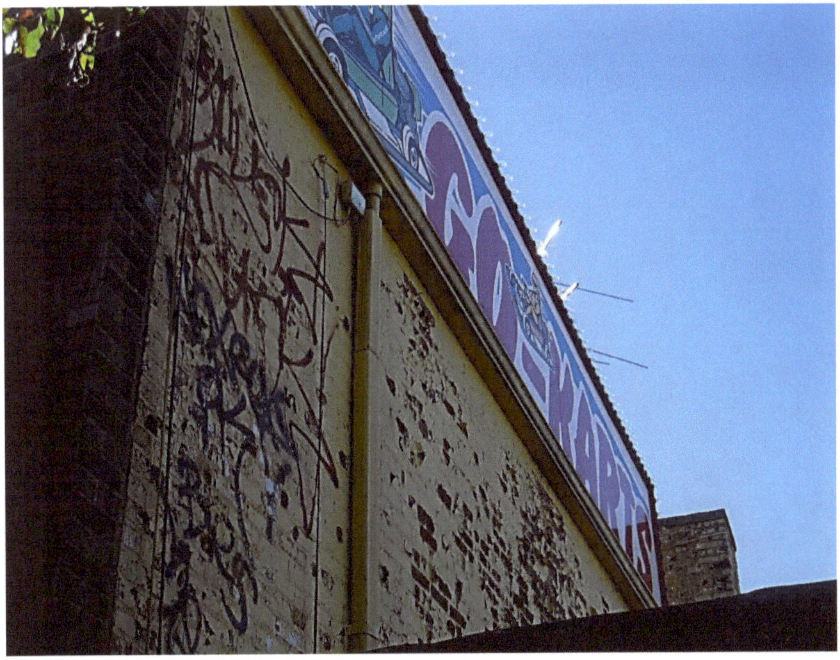

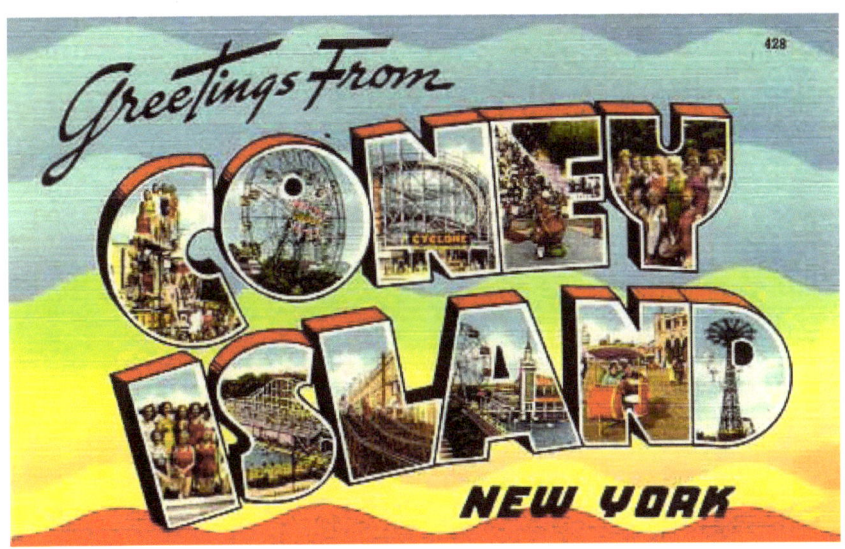

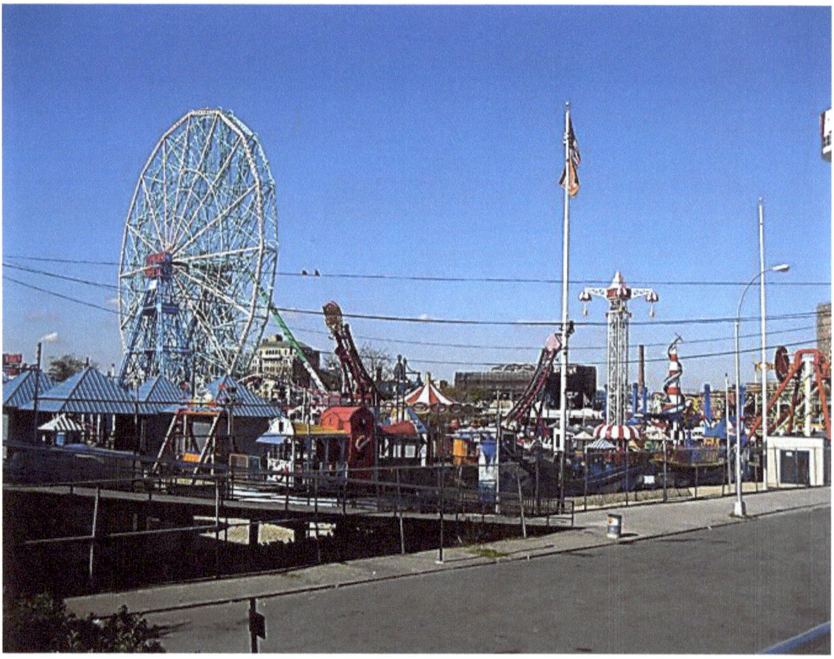

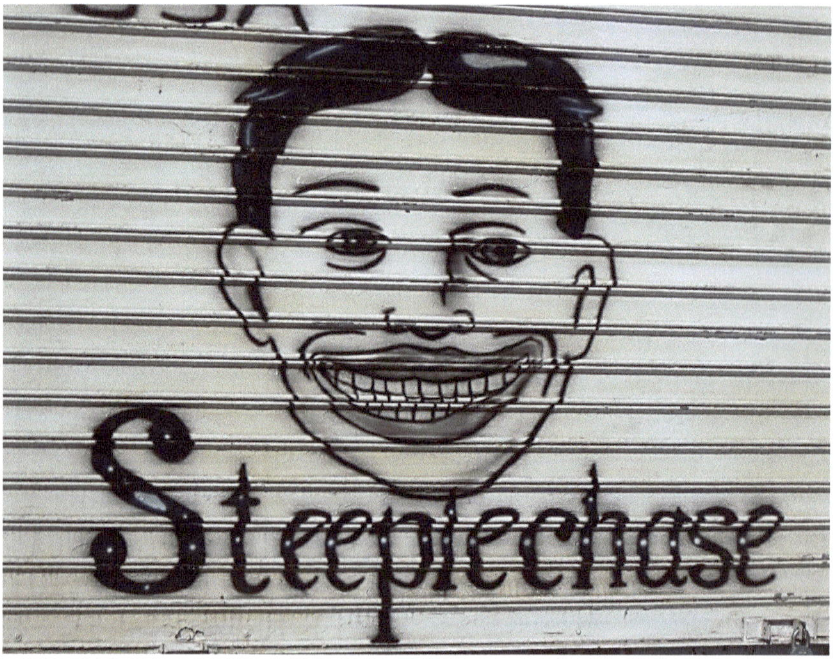
Steeplechase

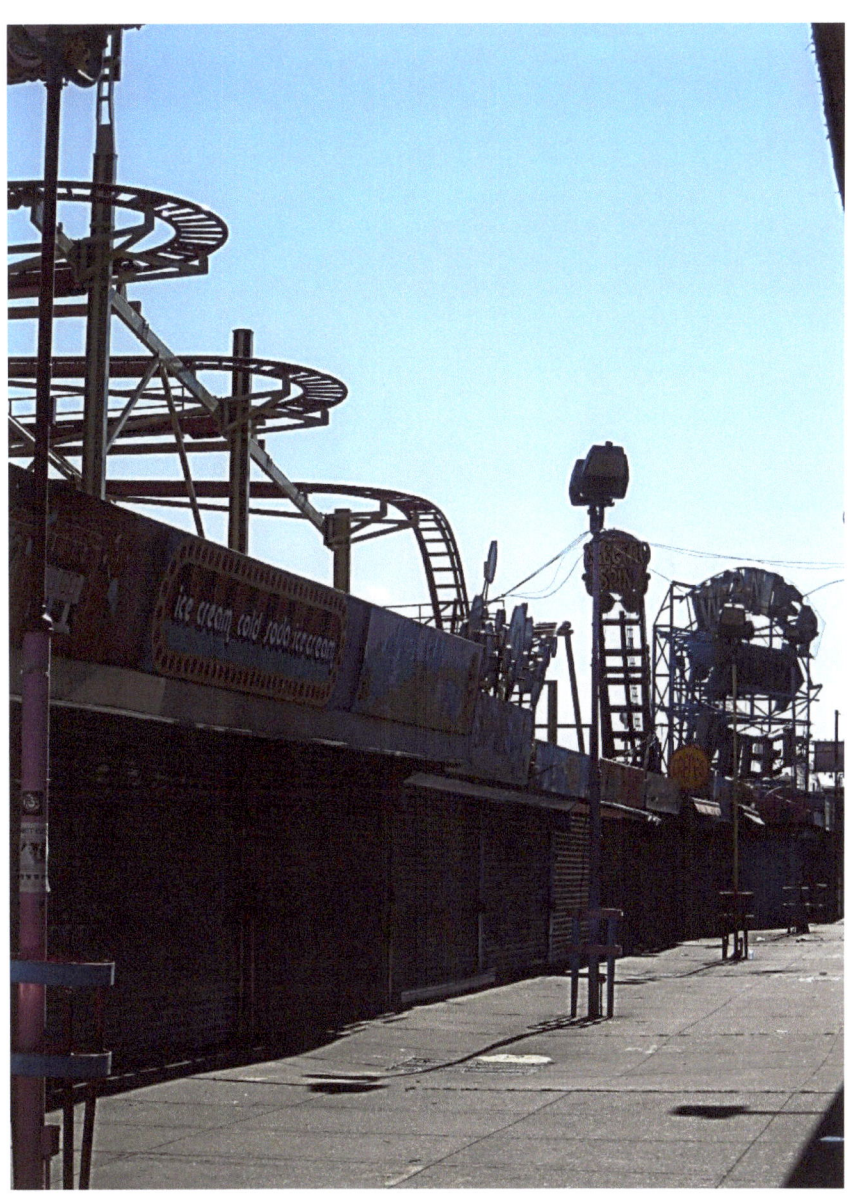

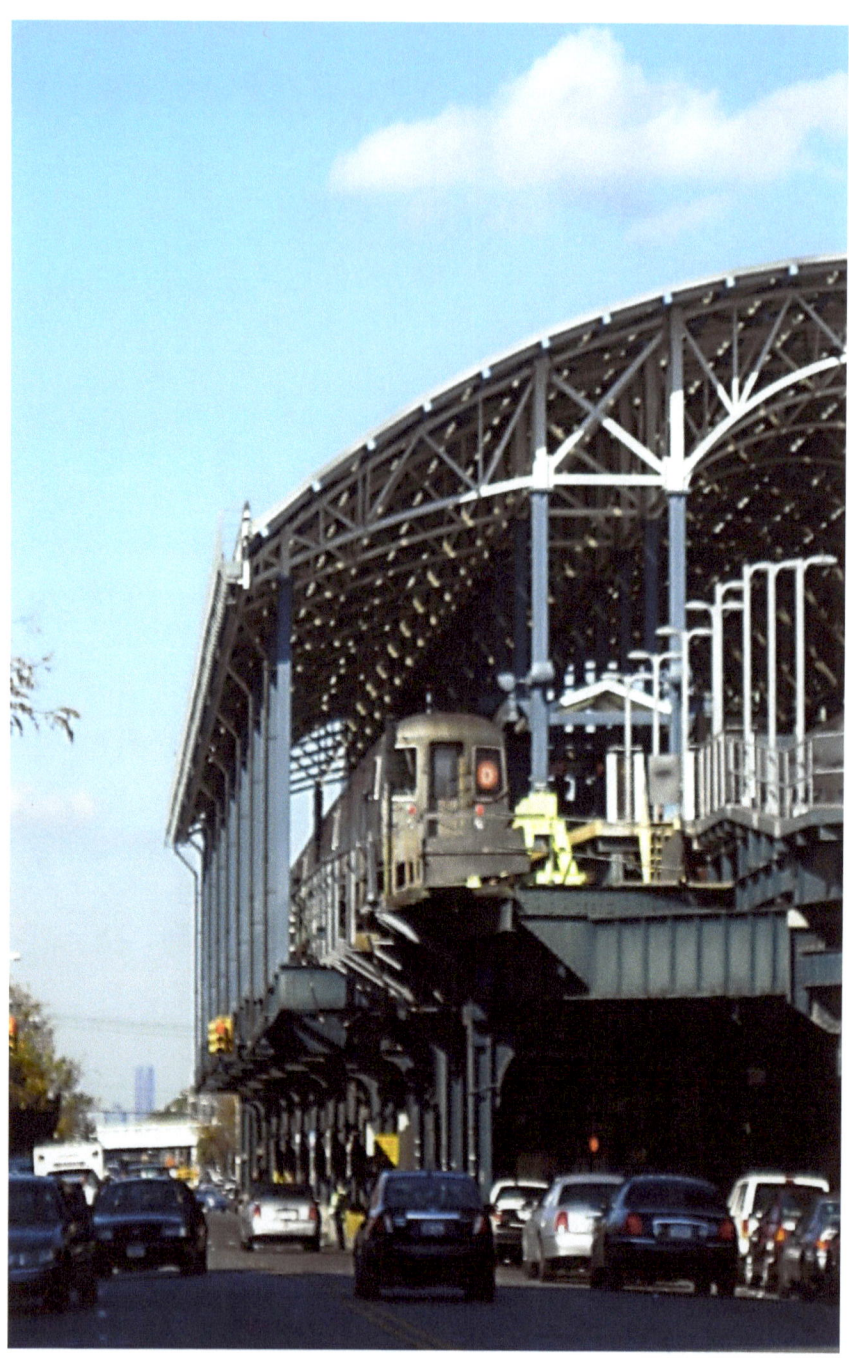

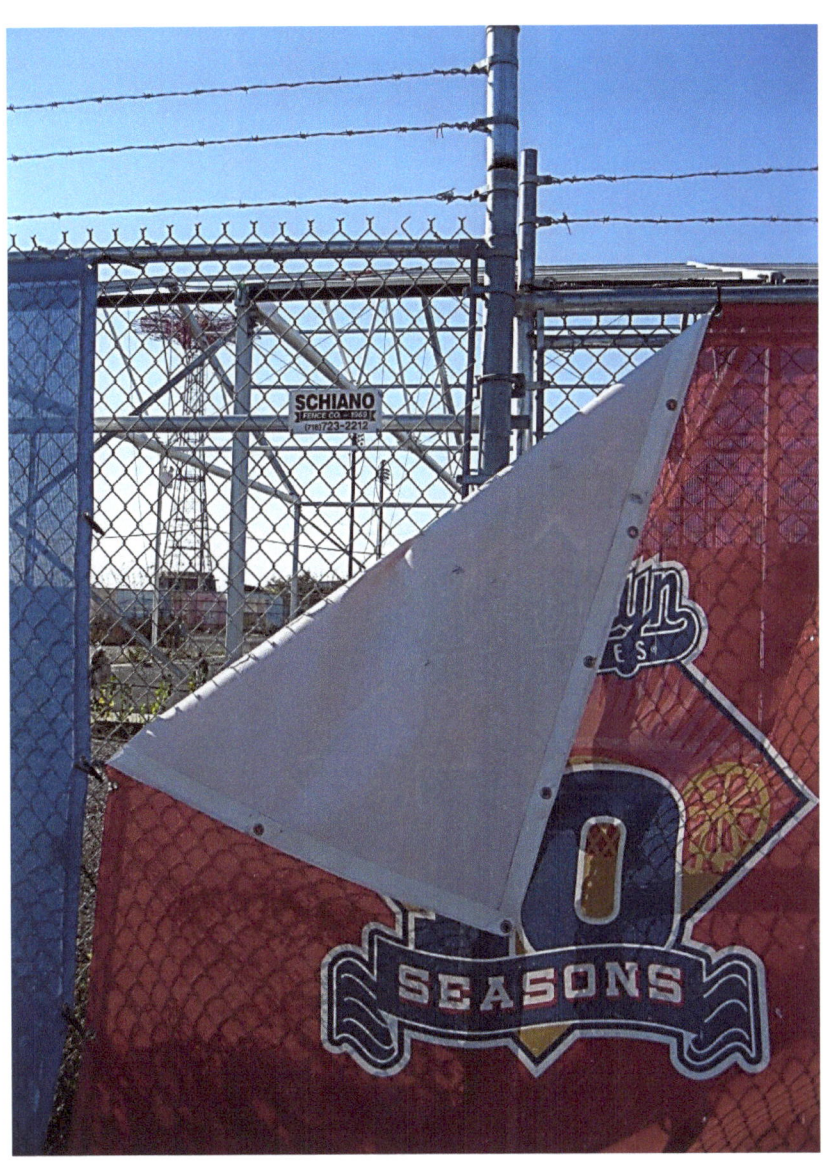

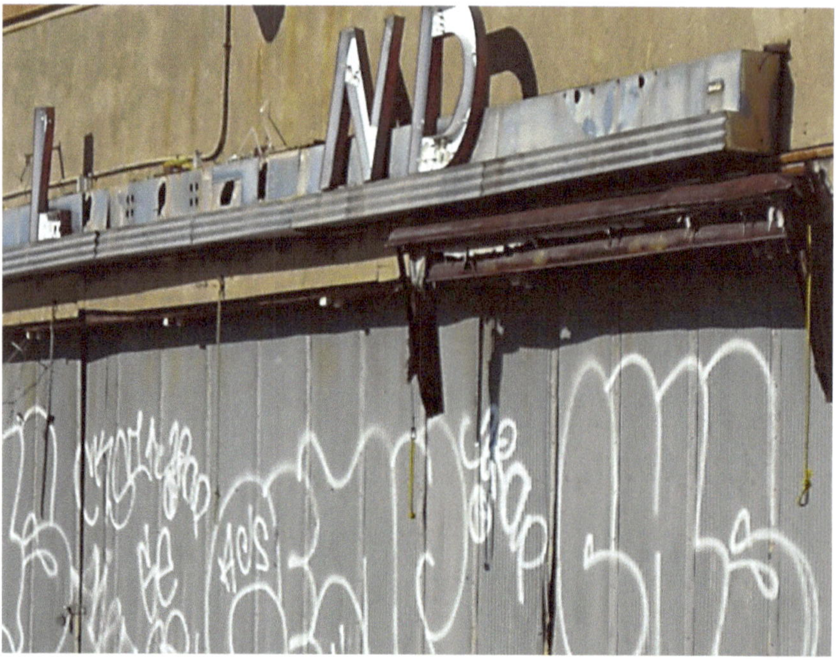

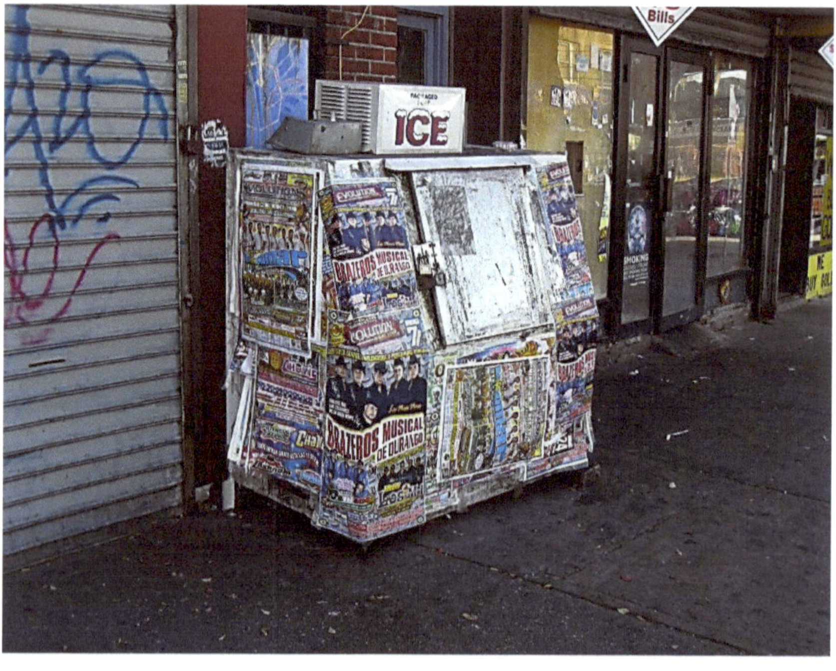
ICE
BRAZEROS MUSICAL DE DURANGO
Bills

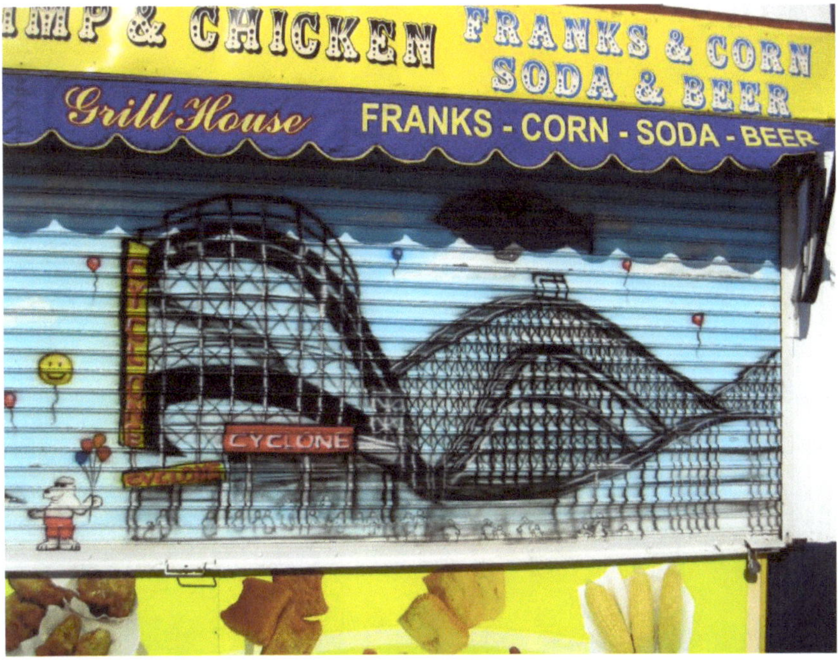

MP & CHICKEN
FRANKS & CORN
SODA & BEER
Grill House
FRANKS - CORN - SODA - BEER
CYCLONE

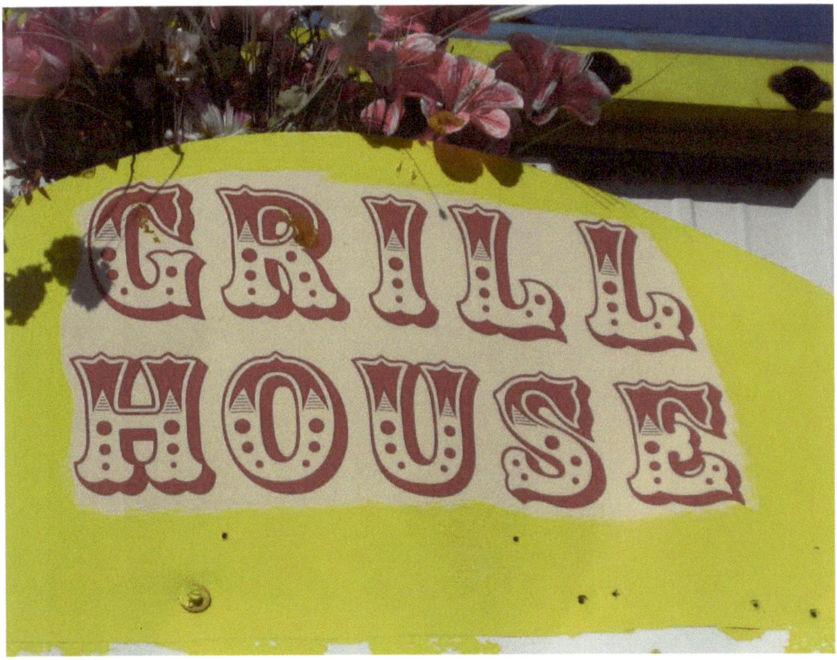

GRILL
HOUSE

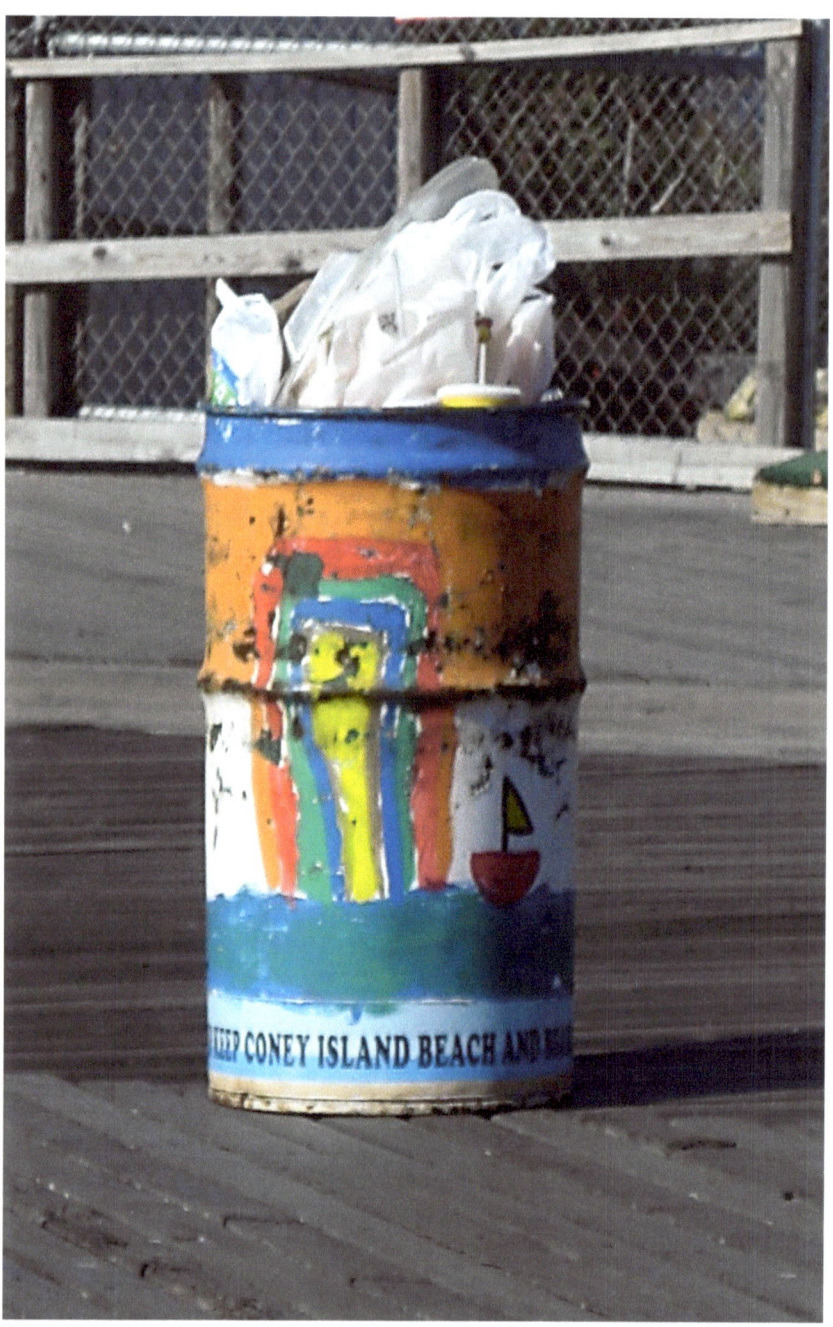

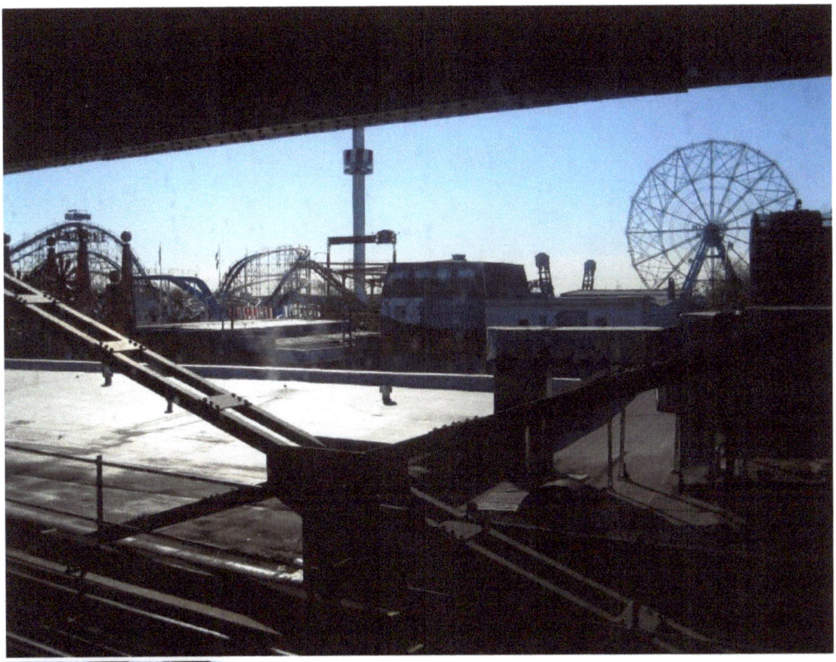

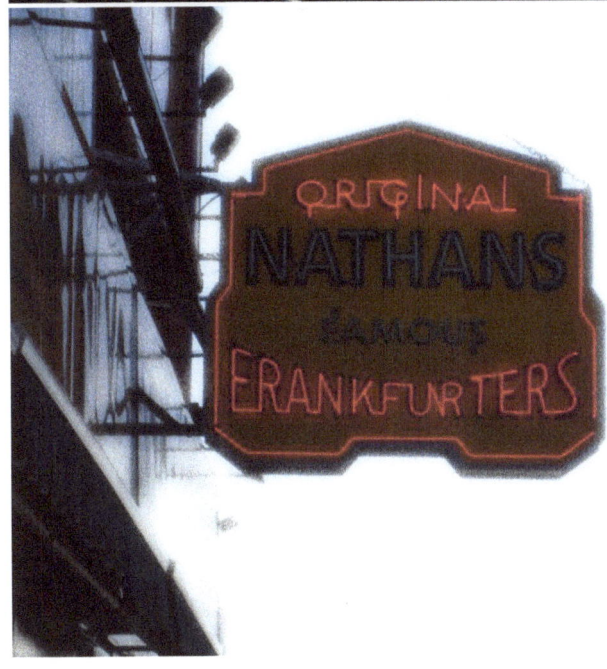

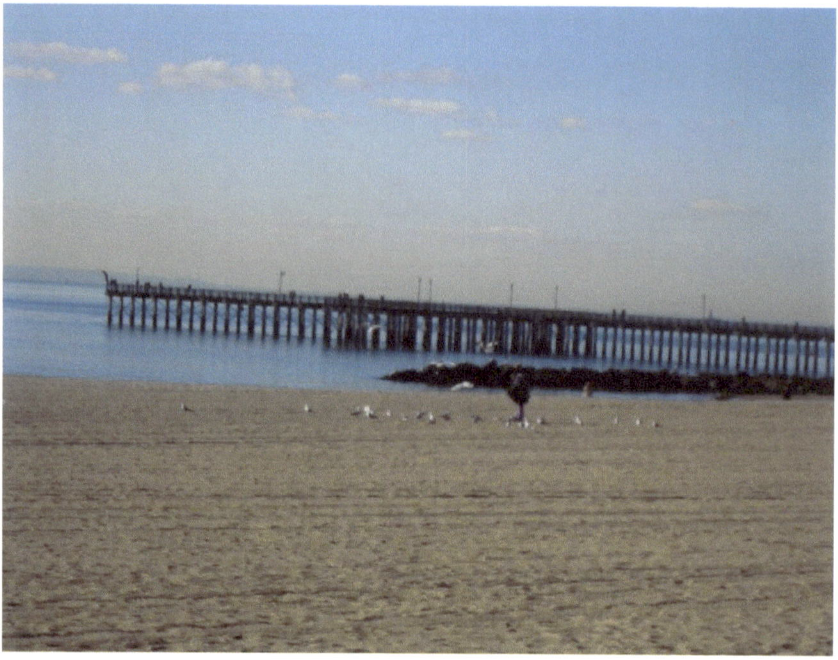

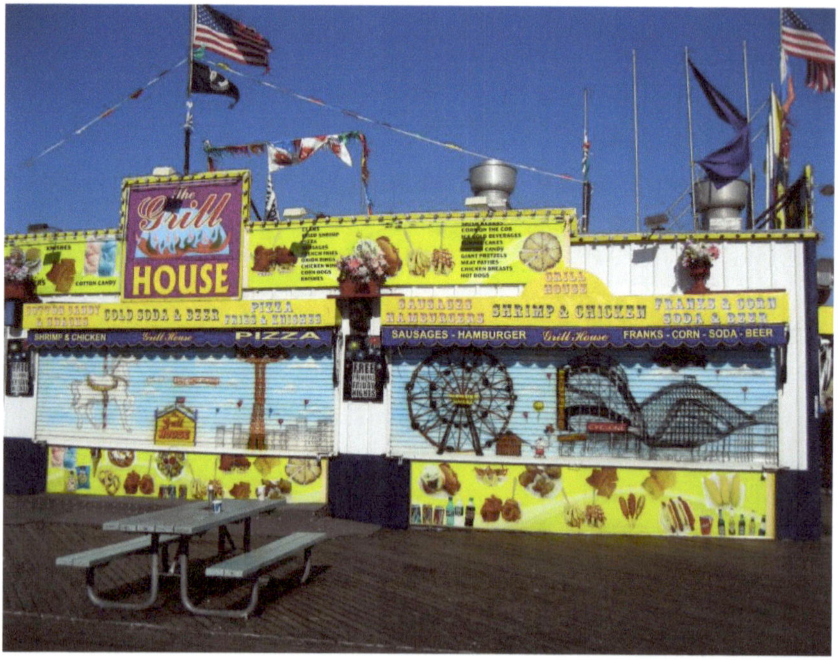
The Grill
HOUSE
COLD SODA & BEER
PIZZA
FRIES & KNISHES
SAUSAGES
HAMBURGERS
SHRIMP & CHICKEN
FRANKS & CORN
SODA & BEER
SHRIMP & CHICKEN
Grill House
PIZZA
SAUSAGES - HAMBURGER
Grill House
FRANKS - CORN - SODA - BEER

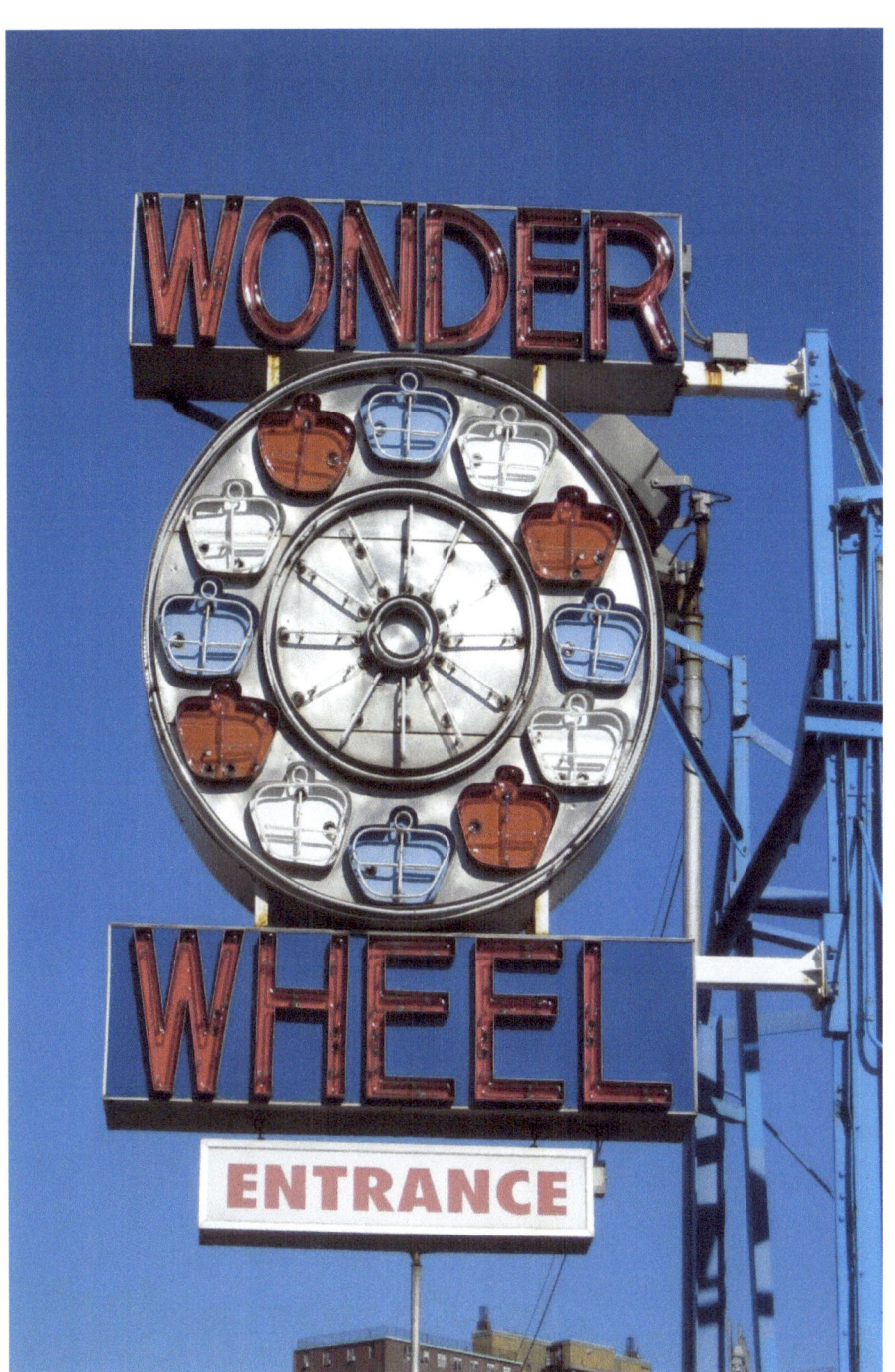

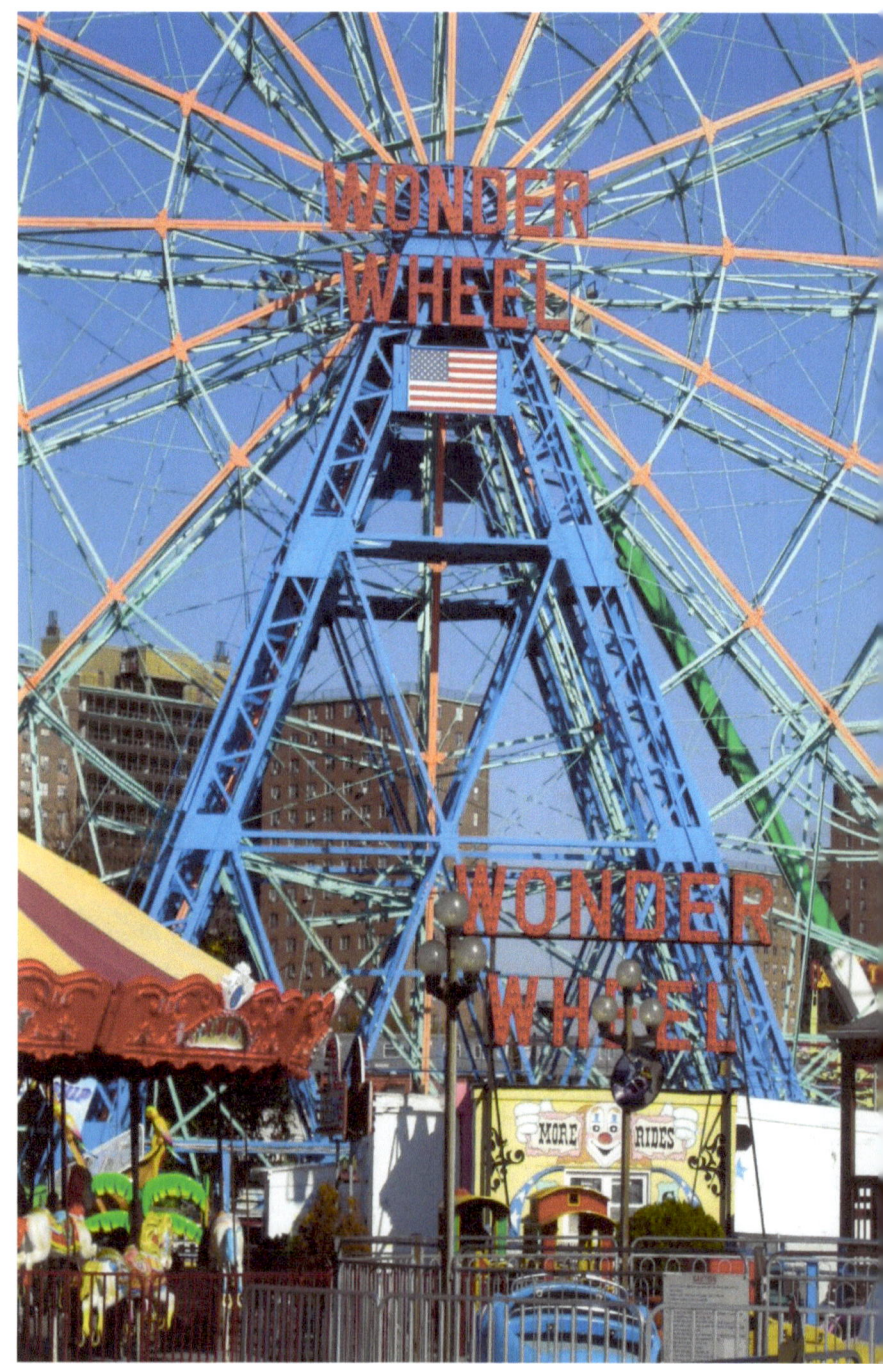

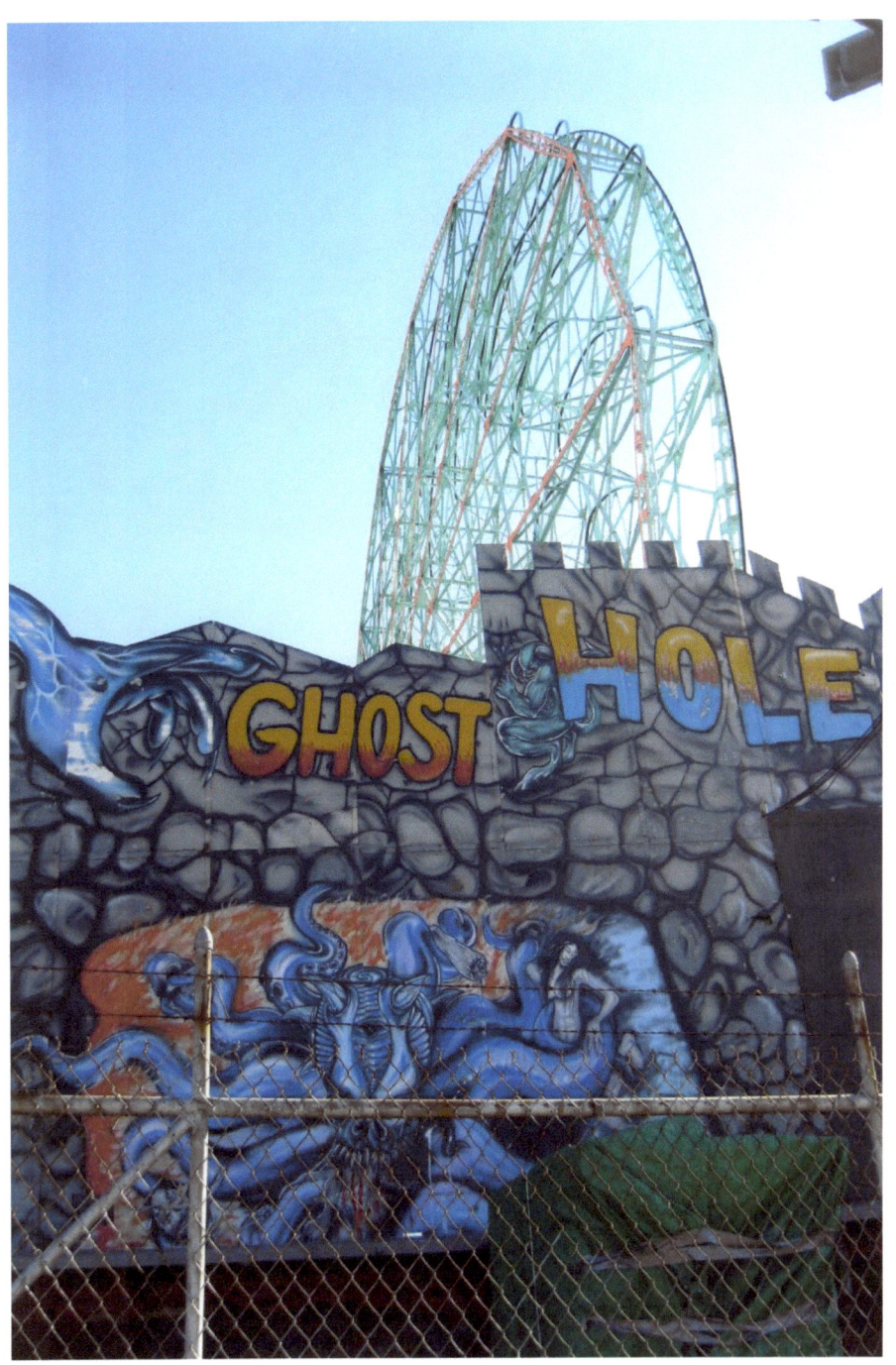

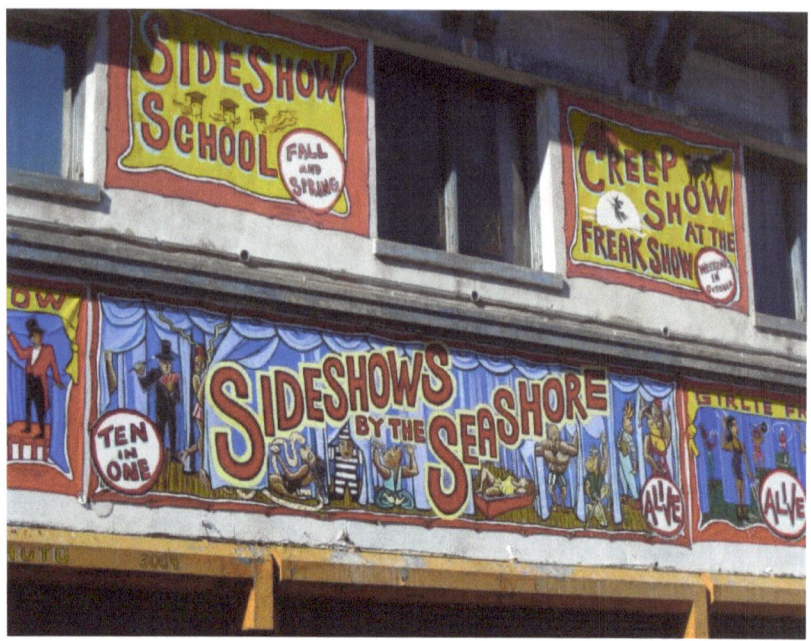

Coney Island has always featured the strange and odd. Sideshows have always been a part of its heritage since its earliest days. Here you would find the bearded lady, pretzel man, the world's strongest man, and lobster boy.

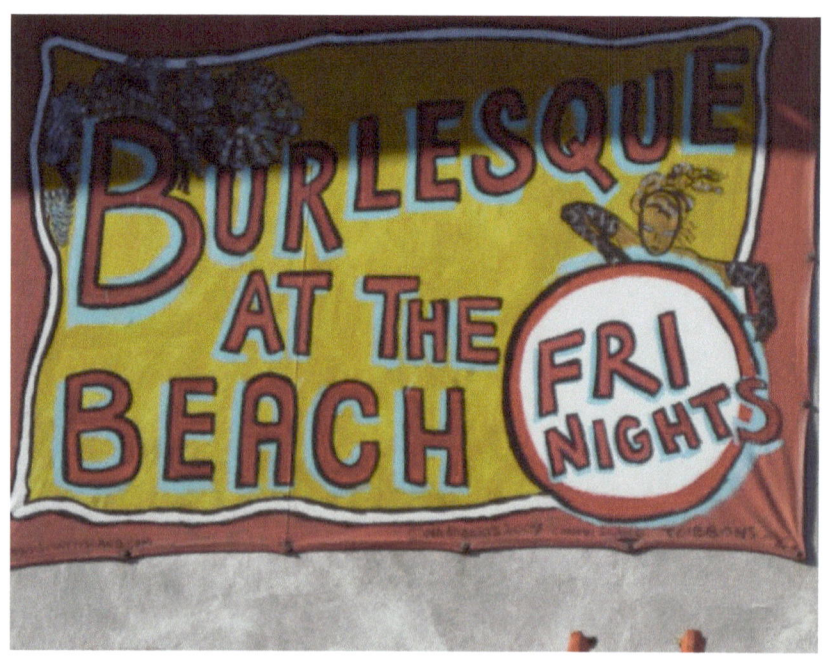

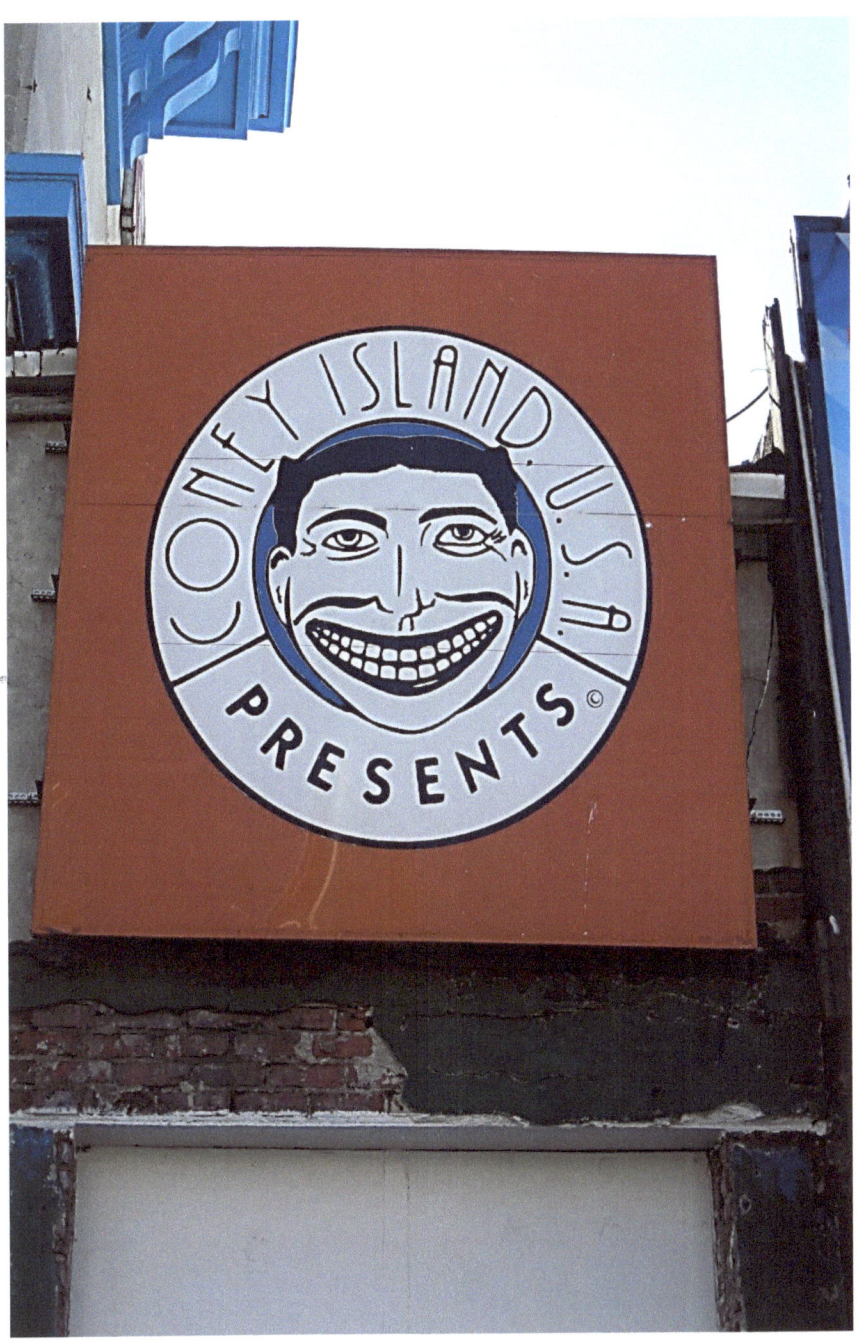

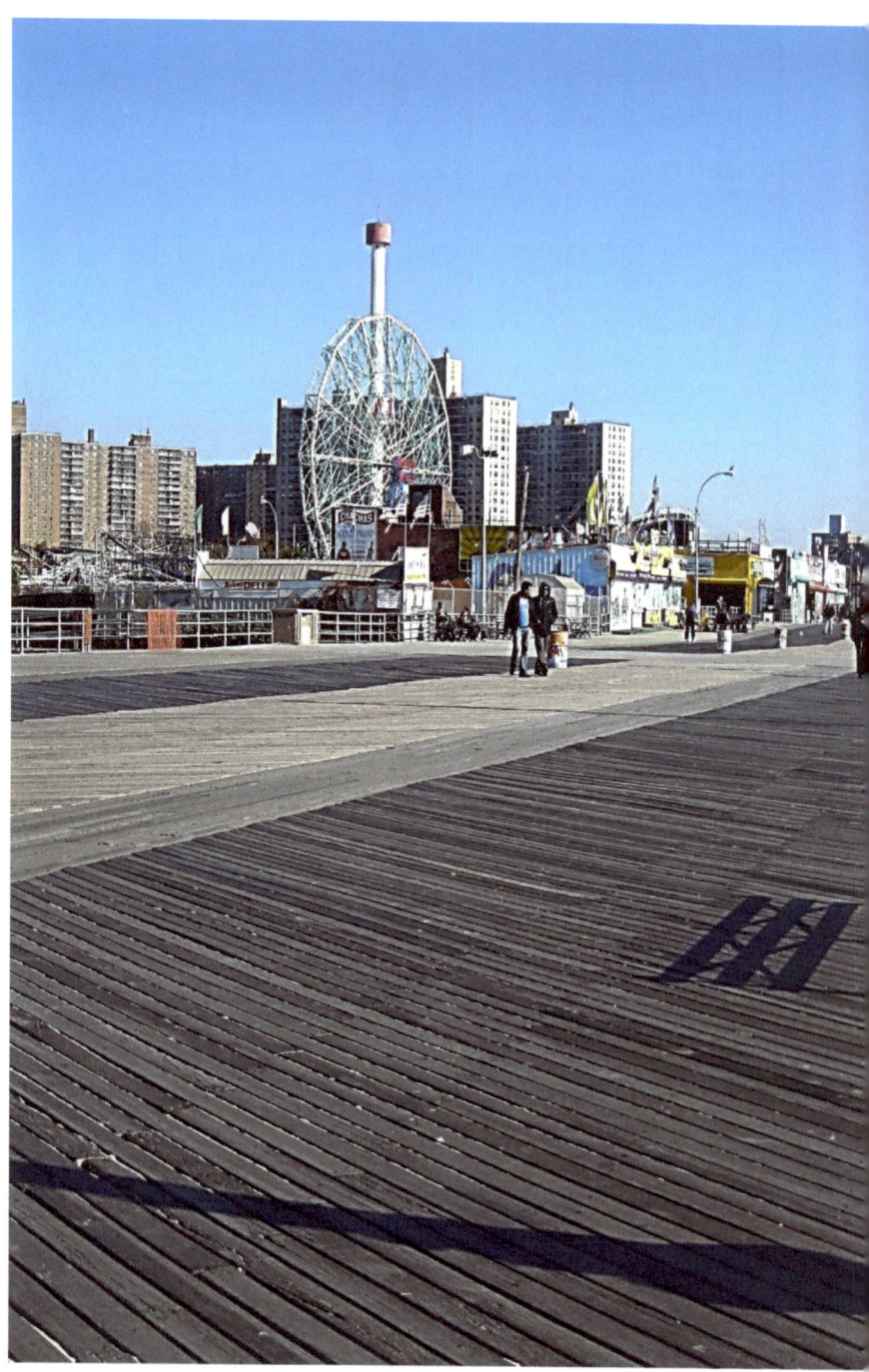

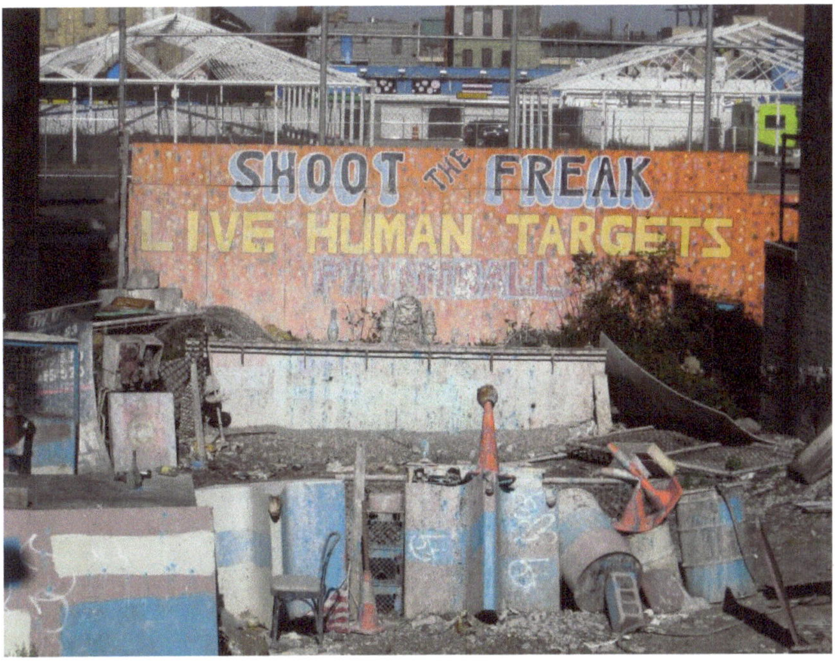
SHOOT THE FREAK
LIVE HUMAN TARGETS

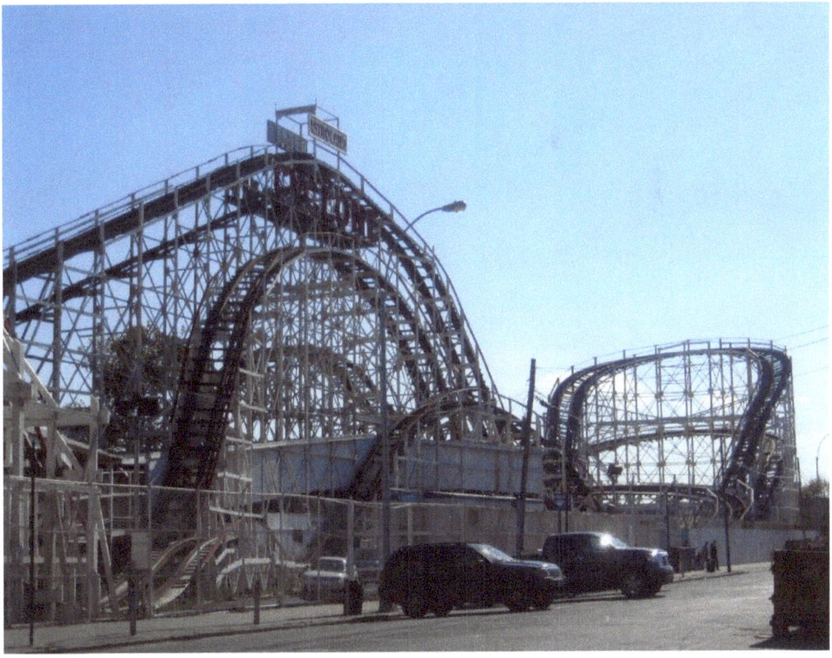

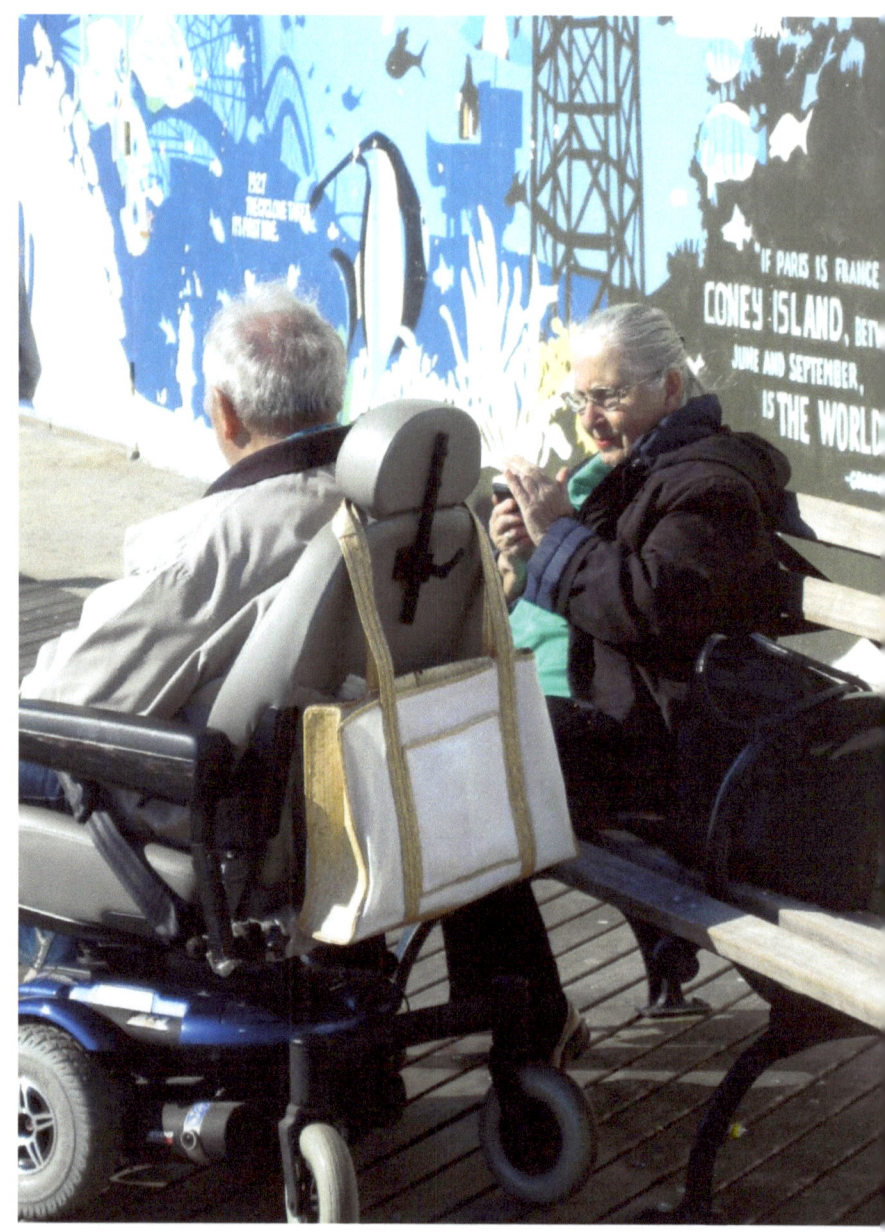

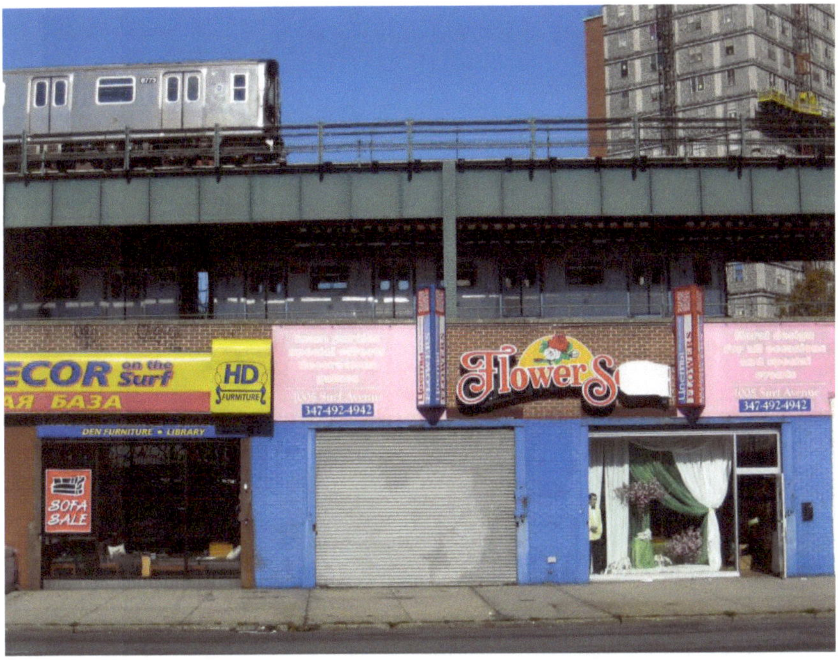
ECOR on the Surf
АЯ БАЗА
HD FURNITURE
DEN FURNITURE • LIBRARY
SOFA SALE
Flower S
347-492-4942
347-492-4942

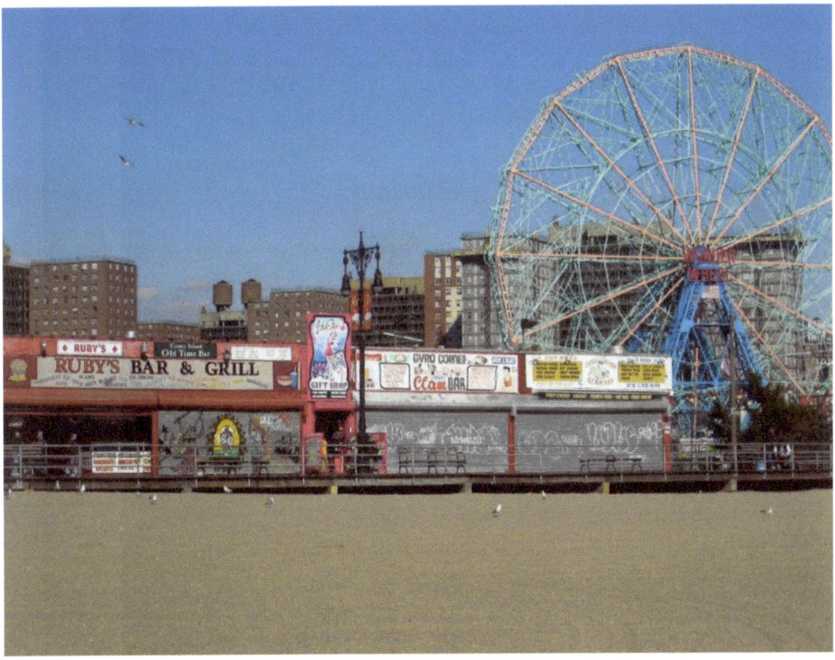
RUBY'S
RUBY'S BAR & GRILL
Old Time Bar
GIFT SHOP
GYRO CORNER
Clam BAR

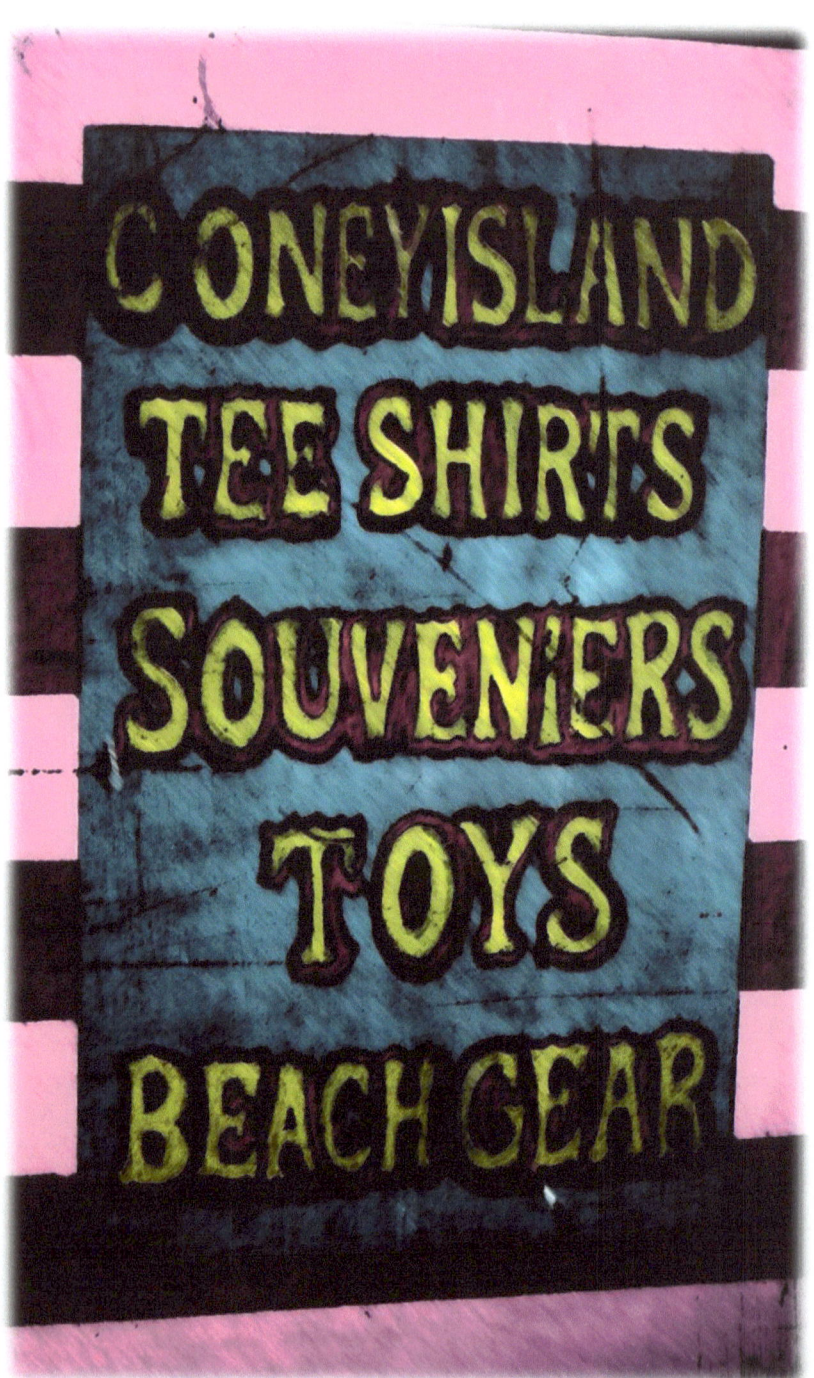

Luna Park
(1903-1946)

Dreamland
(1904-1911)

Steeplechase Park
(1897-1964)

Astroland
(1962-2007)

B & B Carousel
(1935-2004)